gifts from your scrap basket

gifts from your scrap basket

25 patchwork, appliqué and quilting projects for special occasions

GAIL LAWTHER

COLLINS & BROWN

First published in Great Britain in 2000 by
Collins & Brown Ltd
London House
Great Eastern Wharf
Parkgate Road
London SW11 4NQ

Distributed in the United States and Canada by Sterling Publishing Co, 387 Park Avenue South,
New York, NY 10016, USA

Editorial Director: Sarah Hoggett
Editors: Janet Swarbrick and Katie Hardwicke
Designer: Maggie Aldred
Photographer: Jon Stewart
Stylist: Barbara Stewart
Illustrator: Anthony Duke

ISBN 1-85585-826-6 (hardback)
ISBN 1-85585-861-4 (paperback)

British Library Cataloguing-in-Publication Data:
A catalogue record for this title is available from the British Library.

1 3 5 7 9 8 6 4 2

Colour reproduction by Classic Scan Pte Ltd, Singapore
Printed and bound in Hong Kong by Dai Nippon Printing Co Ltd

Illustrated Library.com
Enjoyed this book? For more on this and other great topics,
visit *Illustrated Library* – all your favourite subjects on one website.
http://www.illustratedlibrary.com

CONTENTS

INTRODUCTION

Everybody loves a celebration, and I'm no exception; a chance to get together with friends, to throw a party, to give a present, or simply to wish someone well in a new job or a new house. Whether it's a birthday, a wedding anniversary or the arrival of a new baby, there's always some special occasion just waiting to peep over the horizon. And what could be nicer than to mark the special day with a present or card that you've created yourself?

Just because a present is stitched, it doesn't mean that it has to take forever to make. In this

Above: Birthday card (see page 10)
Opposite page: Knotwork picture (see page 32)

book you'll find a whole range of different gift ideas that will suit just about every occasion, but you'll find that they suit just about every timetable too! Glance at your calendar and realize that it's a friend's birthday next week: no problem – create the cake card on page 10 in a matter of minutes, or put together a gift bag (see page 18) to give a little present with a big impact. Just found out that a new baby's on the way? Make a soft jazzy play-ball (see page 66), or create the wholecloth pram quilt on page 70 in soft baby colours.

At the other end of the scale, maybe a special wedding is coming up in a few months: that gives you plenty of time to stitch the knotwork picture on page 32, or to create the pretty shadow-work bed quilt on page 36.

Because you only need small amounts of fabric for many of these projects, most of them can be created out of your existing fabric stash or scrap basket. None of us ever wants to throw away all those little bits left over when we've finished a large project; now you can be vindicated by using some of them up to create the lovely presents and cards in this book. Don't feel that you have to stick rigidly to the fabrics I've used; for many of the projects I've suggested some ideas for varying the basic design, and you'll probably have lots more of your own.

All the projects use very simple, straightforward techniques, and each project is shown being put together step by step, so that you can see every stage clearly. Any time a special technique is used, such as the trapunto used for

creating the anniversary cards on page 60 or the foundation piecing used for the photograph album cover on page 44, the method is explained in detail within the instructions. The templates given are either full sized, or the enlargement factor is mentioned in the instructions; simply take the page along to a local library or copy shop and make a photocopy at the enlargement specified in the project.

Whether your taste is for the traditional or the modern, I hope that you'll find all kinds of projects in this book that will be just what you're looking for to make your own celebration days really special.

BIRTHDAYS

Looking for a special way to wish someone 'many happy returns'? Try one of the projects in this section. The birthday card featuring a fancy cake complete with candles is ideal for any age; the drawstring gift bag is great for a small or hard-to-wrap present; and if making pretty cakes isn't your strength, buy one ready-made and iced, and add an appliquéd and beaded cake ribbon for colour and decoration.

PROJECTS:
Birthday Card
Technique: *machine appliqué*

Cake Ribbon
Techniques: *machine appliqué,
hand appliqué, beading*

Gift Bag
Techniques: *machine appliqué,
machine sewing*

Birthday Card

A SCRUMPTIOUS CAKE MAKES AN excellent birthday card design for any recipient, whatever their age! The design is built up in simple machine appliqué, and the machine stitching creates extra decoration on the cake icing. Why not make several cards in one sitting? Then you've always got a special card ready for the next birthday that comes along. Try the card in different colour combinations – green or red or purple for the cake-stand, with toning candles, for instance. Or use a piece of dark brown fabric to create a chocolate cake instead of a sponge! You could also make this design work very well for a silver, gold or any other anniversary, by picking suitable colours and adding appropriate trimmings such as ribbons, beads or lace.

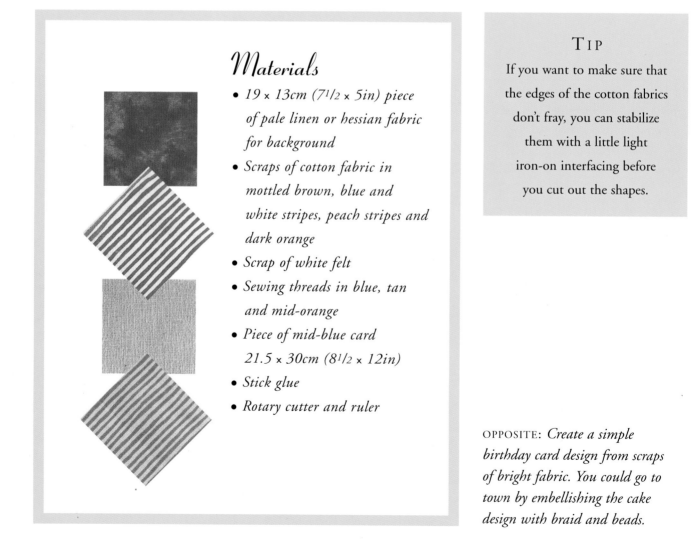

Materials

- *19 x 13cm (7¹/2 x 5in) piece of pale linen or hessian fabric for background*
- *Scraps of cotton fabric in mottled brown, blue and white stripes, peach stripes and dark orange*
- *Scrap of white felt*
- *Sewing threads in blue, tan and mid-orange*
- *Piece of mid-blue card 21.5 x 30cm (8¹/2 x 12in)*
- *Stick glue*
- *Rotary cutter and ruler*

TIP

If you want to make sure that the edges of the cotton fabrics don't fray, you can stabilize them with a little light iron-on interfacing before you cut out the shapes.

OPPOSITE: *Create a simple birthday card design from scraps of bright fabric. You could go to town by embellishing the cake design with braid and beads.*

Making the Birthday Card

1 *Trace or photocopy the templates on page 13. Cut one cake piece from the mottled brown fabric, one cake-stand from the blue and white striped fabric, and one icing shape from the white felt.* INSET: *Trim the edges of the background fabric with pinking shears.*

2 *Pin the cake-stand piece onto the background. Set your machine to a small zigzag and thread it with the blue thread. Stitch down the sides and around the bottom of the cake-stand section (you don't need to stitch across the top as this will be covered).*

3 *Pin the cake piece in position just overlapping the top of the cake-stand and appliqué it in the same way as Step 2, using the tan thread. Again, you need only to stitch down the sides and along the bottom edge.*

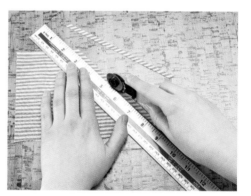

4 *Use a rotary cutter and ruler to cut a 5-mm (¹/4-in) strip at 45° across the peach fabric, then cut three 3-cm (1¹/4-in) lengths from this and curve the top edges slightly. (Alternatively, use the candle template to cut three candles at a 45° angle.)*

5 *Pin the candles in position about 5mm (¹/4in) above the cake section, spacing them evenly, and stitch around the sides and top edges using orange thread.*

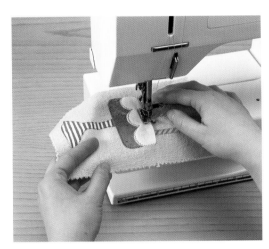

6 *Pin the icing shape over the top of the cake section and work orange zigzag all the way around the shape, finishing off the stitching neatly when the circuit is complete.*

7 *Cut three flame shapes from the orange fabric and pin them in position at the tops of the candles.* INSET: *Set your machine to straight stitch, and stitch a line down the centre of each flame. Pull the threads to the back to finish them neatly.*

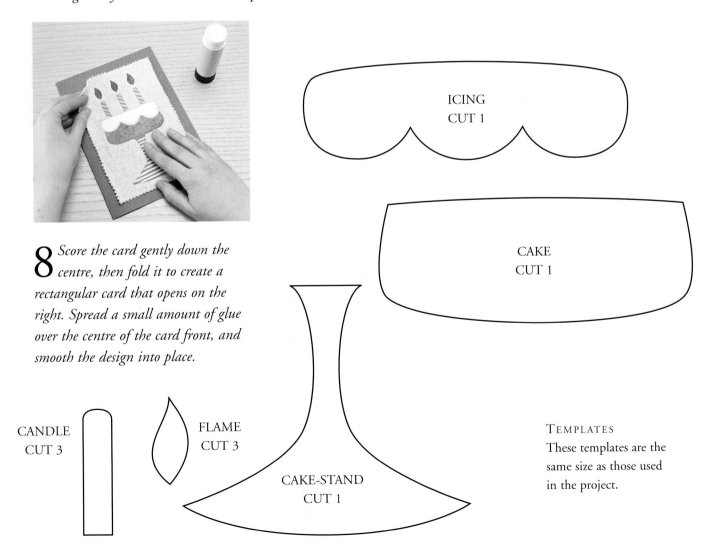

8 *Score the card gently down the centre, then fold it to create a rectangular card that opens on the right. Spread a small amount of glue over the centre of the card front, and smooth the design into place.*

ICING
CUT 1

CAKE
CUT 1

CANDLE
CUT 3

FLAME
CUT 3

CAKE-STAND
CUT 1

TEMPLATES
These templates are the same size as those used in the project.

Cake Ribbon

$\mathcal{N}$O GOOD AT CAKE ICING? Cheat instead; add colour and decoration to a bought cake by stitching a zingy cake ribbon, embellished with simple appliqué and metallic beads. Measure the circumference of your cake, then add about 5cm (2in) for overlap; pin the finished ribbon on the cake, then remove the pin to release the ribbon before cutting. You can use the bright colours shown here, or adapt the colour scheme to suit different occasions – for instance, pick out colours from a bridal bouquet, or work in appropriate shades and materials for a silver, gold or ruby wedding anniversary.

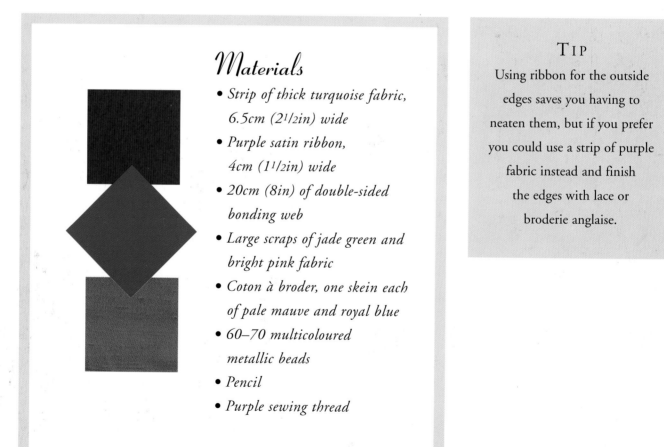

Materials
- *Strip of thick turquoise fabric, 6.5cm (2¹/2in) wide*
- *Purple satin ribbon, 4cm (1¹/2in) wide*
- *20cm (8in) of double-sided bonding web*
- *Large scraps of jade green and bright pink fabric*
- *Coton à broder, one skein each of pale mauve and royal blue*
- *60–70 multicoloured metallic beads*
- *Pencil*
- *Purple sewing thread*

TIP
Using ribbon for the outside edges saves you having to neaten them, but if you prefer you could use a strip of purple fabric instead and finish the edges with lace or broderie anglaise.

OPPOSITE: *A glitzy ribbon turns a simple cake into a centrepiece worthy of any birthday spread; choose the colours of your fabrics and beads to complement the cake's decoration.*

Making the Cake Ribbon

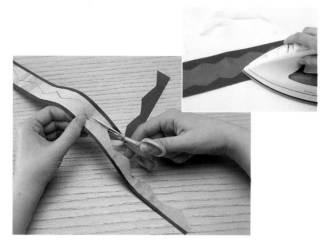

1 *Cut a turquoise fabric strip to the circumference of your cake plus 5cm (2in). Cut 2.5cm (1in) wide strips of bonding web to total the same length. On the paper side of the bonding web strip(s), trace the zigzag line (page 17) down the centre. INSET: Lay the purple ribbon, right side down, on the ironing board. Place the bonding web, paper side up, down the centre of the ribbon. Fuse into place.*

2 *Cut along the zigzag lines to create two saw-tooth strips of ribbon. Lay the fabric strip, right side up, on the ironing board. INSET: Peel the backing papers from the pieces of ribbon and lay them, right sides up, down the sides of the turquoise strip. Place the points of the zigzags opposite each other and roughly 2.5cm (1in) apart. Fuse them into place.*

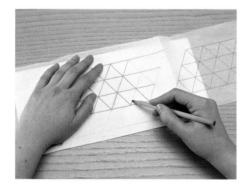

3 *Trace the triangle design (page 17) twice onto the paper side of the remaining bonding web. Cut out the two pieces. Fuse one onto the back of the jade green fabric and the other onto the back of the pink fabric.*

4 *Cut out the triangles along the marked lines. Peel off the backing papers and fuse alternate pink and green triangles in the spaces created by the purple zigzags.*

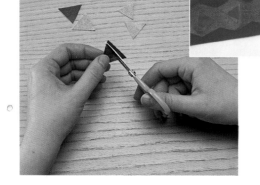

5 *Cut about 2mm (1/8in) off one side of each remaining triangle to make them slightly smaller. INSET: Position a small green triangle on top of each large pink one, turning the top one slightly, and fuse into shape. Do the same with the smaller pink triangles on top of the larger green ones.*

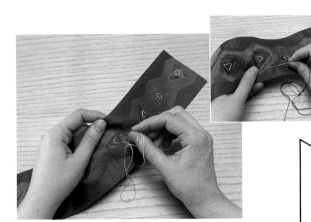

TEMPLATES
These templates are the
same size as those used in
the project.

Zigzag line

6 *Using the pale mauve coton à broder, make three large straight stitches on each of the central triangles to secure them.* INSET: *Using royal blue coton à broder, make a long straight stitch down each edge of each zigzag on the purple ribbon edges.*

7 *Stitch a bead into position just in from the tip of each zigzag shape, then scatter the other beads randomly along the turquoise fabric.*

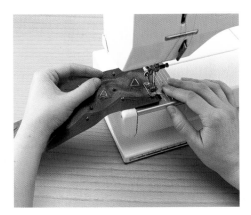

TRIANGLE DESIGN: CUT 2

8 *Thread your sewing machine with purple thread and set it to a small zigzag. Turn under the raw edge at the beginning of the ribbon and stitch it down by machine to make a straight edge. Pin the ribbon onto the cake with the neatened end overlapping the raw edge.*

Gift Bag

MAKE YOUR GIFT-WRAPPING stand out from the crowd; stitch a velvet gift bag decorated with party balloons. It's a good way of solving the problem of an awkward-shaped present, too; just wrap it in tissue paper and pop it inside, then pull the drawstring tight to make sure there's no peeping! Use this pattern to create a bag in white silk or velvet to hold a wedding present, perhaps decorating the bag with the couple's initials in appliqué. Or use the birthday cake design on page 13, or one of the anniversary designs on page 63, instead of the balloons.

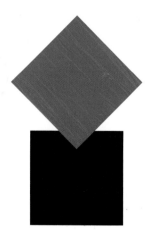

Materials

- 86 × 27cm (34 × 10½in) piece, and two 21.5 × 6.5cm (8½ × 2½in) strips of deep red velvet
- Scraps of cotton or silk fabric in bright pink, yellow stripes and pink/yellow polka dots
- Sewing threads in bright pink and deep yellow, and dark red to match the velvet
- Metallic machine embroidery thread in deep pink
- 36 × 25cm (14 × 10in) piece of Stitch 'n' Tear or white cartridge paper
- 60cm (24in) deep yellow ribbon for the bow
- 140cm (55in) gold-coloured fine cord
- Chalk marker

TIPS

Try to find a furnishing velvet for this project if possible: these often have a fused or bonded backing, which prevents the fraying problems you get with ordinary velvet.

•

If your machine doesn't do a satin stitch, use a close zigzag instead. Try the stitch out on a piece of scrap fabric to see how close you can make the stitches without them snagging.

OPPOSITE: *This velvet bag is almost a present in itself; after the lucky recipient has enjoyed the present inside, the bag can be kept for trinkets or reused for the next birthday!*

Making the Gift Bag

1 *Enlarge the balloon motifs on page 21 by 153% on a photocopier and use these templates to cut three balloon shapes from the scrap fabrics. Cut the central part-balloon in plain pink, the right-hand balloon in the polka-dot fabric, and the left-hand balloon in the yellow striped fabric.*

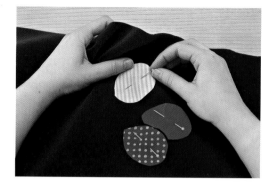

2 *Lay the large piece of velvet right side up on a flat surface; pin the pink balloon so that it is in the centre of the rectangle with its top 20cm (8in) down from the raw edge of the velvet. Pin the other two balloons in position next to it.*

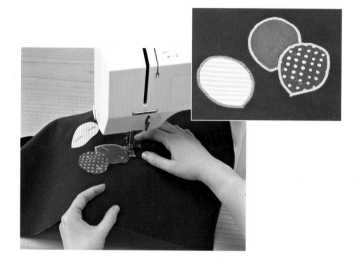

3 *Position the Stitch 'n' Tear or cartridge paper underneath the design and pin it in place. Thread your machine with yellow thread and set it to a medium-width satin stitch. Stitch around the outside edge of the pink balloon, then stitch around the entire outline of the polka-dot balloon.* INSET: *Re-thread the machine with pink thread, and stitch all around the edge of the striped balloon in the same way.*

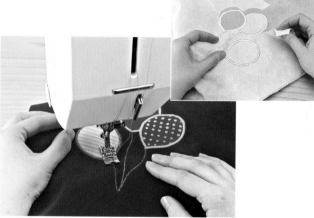

4 *Set the machine to a narrow satin stitch and re-thread it with pink. Use the chalk marker to draw in three balloon strings, all going down to the same meeting point at the bottom of the design, then stitch over these lines in pink satin stitch.* INSET: *Remove the pieces of Stitch 'n' Tear or foundation paper by pulling them gently away from the stitching.*

5 *Use the chalk marker to draw in squiggles for the streamers (you don't need to be too accurate about the exact positioning of these). Thread your machine with the metallic thread and set it to straight stitch, drop the feed dogs and put on the embroidery foot. Stitch loosely over each squiggle three or four times, moving the fabric under the machine to create the streamer shapes.*

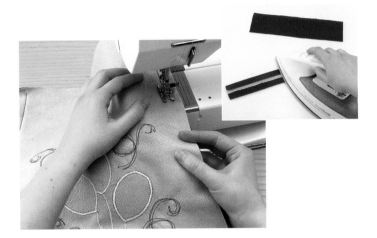

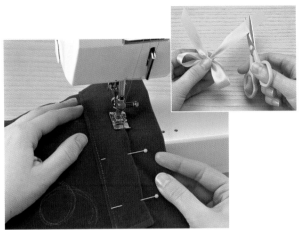

6 Fold the large piece of velvet in half, right sides together, and stitch a 1.5-cm (1/2-in) seam down each side. Clip the bottom corners and turn out the bag shape. INSET: Fold under and press 1.5cm (1/2in) down each long edge of the velvet casing strips. Fold each end under 1.5cm (1/2in) and stitch by machine.

7 Fold the top 7.5cm (3in) of the velvet inside the bag. Pin a casing strip to the front and back, with the lower edges of the strips 6.5cm (2 1/2in) down from the top fold. Stitch by machine along the top and bottom edges of each strip. INSET: Make a bow in the ribbon and pull it tightly to secure the knot. Trim the edges in a neat diagonal, then stitch the bow by hand to the bottom of the balloon strings, catching in the back of the bow with a few stitches.

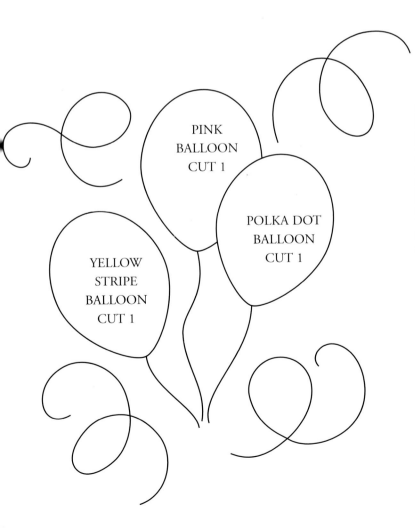

PINK
BALLOON
CUT 1

POLKA DOT
BALLOON
CUT 1

YELLOW
STRIPE
BALLOON
CUT 1

8 Thread a double loop of the cord through the casings and tie the ends together at one side. Pop your present inside, and pull up the drawstring!

TEMPLATE
Enlarge the template by 153%
on a photocopier.

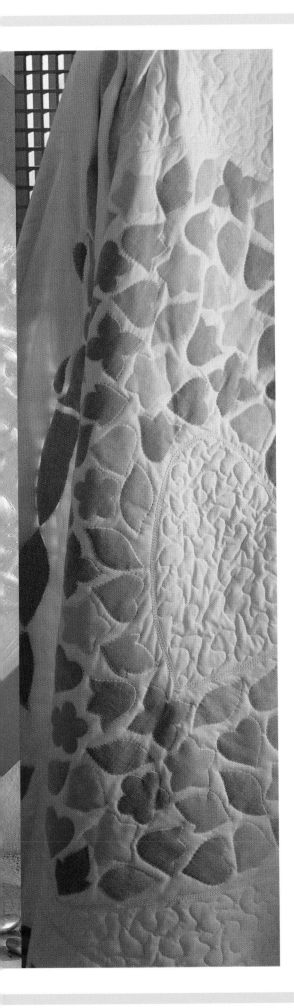

ENGAGEMENTS AND WEDDINGS

Make the big day one that the couple will never forget, with these ideas for unique presents. The interweaving Celtic knot is particularly suitable for an engagement or marriage celebration; the ivory fabrics used for the ring cushion should blend into any bride's colour-scheme and the romantic doves card would be suitable as an engagement congratulations. To create a real heirloom, use up some bright fabrics to make a quilt decorated with a heart-shaped garland of confetti pieces.

PROJECTS:

Ring Cushion
Techniques: *crazy patchwork by machine, machine sewing, hand embroidery, beading*

Doves Card
Technique: *hand appliqué*

Knotwork Picture
Techniques: *hand embroidery, trapunto quilting*

Confetti Quilt
Techniques: *shadow quilting, machine sewing, free machine quilting*

Ring Cushion

A CRAZY PATCHWORK PIECE in exotic fabrics makes an unusual ring cushion to be carried by a small bridesmaid or pageboy. Stitch the cushion in white and ivory fabrics, decorated with white embroidery and pearl beads, or make it from scraps of fabric to match the bride's and bridesmaids' dresses or the groom's waistcoat. You can embellish the cushion with a selection of pretty embroidery stitches, such as herringbone, single or double feather stitch and zigzag chain stitch.

Materials

- *Two 41cm (16in) squares of firm white fabric*
- *Large scraps of 7–8 different white or ivory fabrics, some plain and some textured*
- *One skein of white stranded embroidery cotton*
- *White sewing thread*
- *White or ivory pearl beads*
- *60cm (24in) of fine white or silver ribbon*
- *Pack of polyester filling*

TIP

Don't stitch the beads too close to the edges of the design, or they will get caught up when you stitch the seam.

OPPOSITE: *A ring cushion adds a perfect finishing touch to a special day and is a beautiful keepsake that can be treasured along with many happy memories.*

Making the Ring Cushion

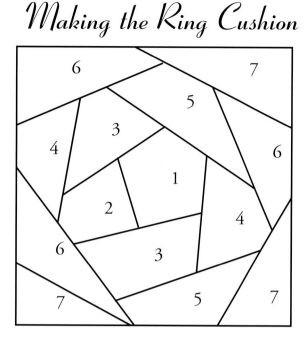

ORDER OF ASSEMBLY
You can add your pieces randomly, or follow the rough sequence shown here to produce a design similar to the cushion in the photograph.

1 *Lay one of the squares of white fabric on a flat surface and cut an irregular patch from one of the textured fabrics. Pin the textured patch, right side up, in the centre of the square.*
INSET: *Cut a second patch in a different shape from another fabric. Lay this second patch right side down on top of the central patch so that two raw edges align, and pin in place.*

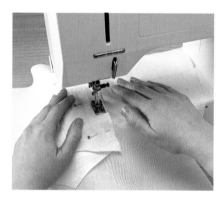

2 *Stitch a 1-cm (1/2-in) seam down the aligned edges with matching thread.*

3 *Fold the second patch to the right side and press.*
INSET: *Cut a third patch and pin it along a different edge of the central patch.*

4 *Add more patches around the central patch and press them open. Continue building up the pattern in the same way, keeping a good mixture of plain and patterned textures across the design, until the foundation square is covered. Trim the edges to make a neat square.*

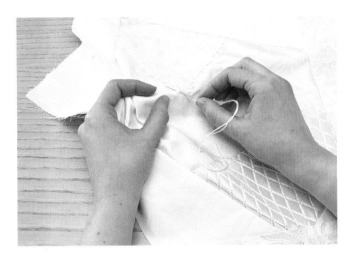

5 *Using three strands of embroidery cotton in the needle, cover each seam with a decorative embroidery stitch. Stitches such as herringbone, single or double feather stitch, blanket stitch and zigzag chain stitch all work well.*

6 *When all the embroidery is complete, stitch on a scattering of pearl beads. You can cluster them at the corners of the patches, as in the photograph, or scatter them randomly across the design.*

8 *Stuff the cushion lightly with polyester filling; don't pad it too firmly – just enough to make it keep its shape. Stitch the opening closed with ladder stitch.*

7 *Lay the embroidered panel and the second square of white fabric right sides together and pin them around the edges. Stitch a 1-cm (1/2-in) seam all round, leaving part of one side open for turning. Trim the seams and clip the corners, then turn the design right side out; press just the very edges of the square to set the seam.*

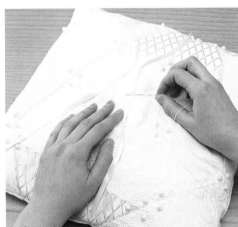

9 *Finally, cut two 30-cm (12-in) lengths of ribbon. Fold each length in half to mark the centre line, then attach each piece to the centre patch of the cushion by taking two or three small stitches across the centre line.*

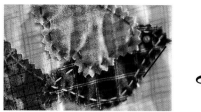

Doves Card

TWO LOVING DOVES convey a message of eternal devotion, perfect as a special card to celebrate an engagement. The folk-art feel of this design is enhanced by the plaid and hessian-type fabrics, and by the bright running stitches used for the appliqué. You could vary the colours to make the same design suit a wedding or a special anniversary, too – or stitch it in different red-and-white prints for Valentine's Day.

Materials

- *20 x 25cm (8 x 10in) piece of pale cream plaid background fabric*
- *Large scraps of fabric in blue plaid, dark cream plaid, brown plaid and red plaid*
- *26 x 30cm (10 x 12in) piece of beige hessian or other loosely woven rustic fabric*
- *Coton à broder in bright yellow, red and blue*
- *2 small red beads*
- *Pinking shears*
- *56 x 33cm (22 x 13in) piece of stiff blue card*
- *8 brown wooden leaf buttons, four large and four small*
- *Stick glue*

TIP

If you find it difficult to cut out accurately with the pinking shears, cut the shapes out first using ordinary scissors, cutting them slightly larger than the templates. Then go around each fabric shape carefully with the pinking shears.

OPPOSITE: *Simple shapes in country prints combine to form a romantic card suitable for an engagement, wedding or anniversary; the romance theme is echoed by the red plaid hearts.*

Making the Doves Card

1 *Trace or photocopy the motifs on page 31 onto stiff card, then cut out the templates. Use the templates to cut shapes from the appropriate fabrics with pinking shears. Cut the two bird shapes from the blue plaid, the two wing shapes from the dark cream plaid, and the two tail shapes from the brown plaid. Cut each shape from the right side of the fabric. Cut two heart shapes, both from the red plaid.*

2 *Trim the rectangle of pale cream plaid with the pinking shears to give it a zigzag edge. Pin the hearts, body shapes and tail pieces onto the background fabric, keeping the plaid lines straight.* INSET: *Add the wing shapes so that they overlap the body pieces.*

3 *Using yellow coton à broder, stitch the body pieces and hearts into position using long, even running stitches.* INSET: *Stitch the tail pieces on in the same way, using red coton à broder, and the wings using blue. Stitch the beads in position to create the doves' eyes.*

4 *Lay the design onto the hessian and trim the hessian with ordinary scissors so that there is an even border all around the design; keep the grain of the hessian straight down the edges. Fray a few threads out from each side of the hessian to create a small fringe.*

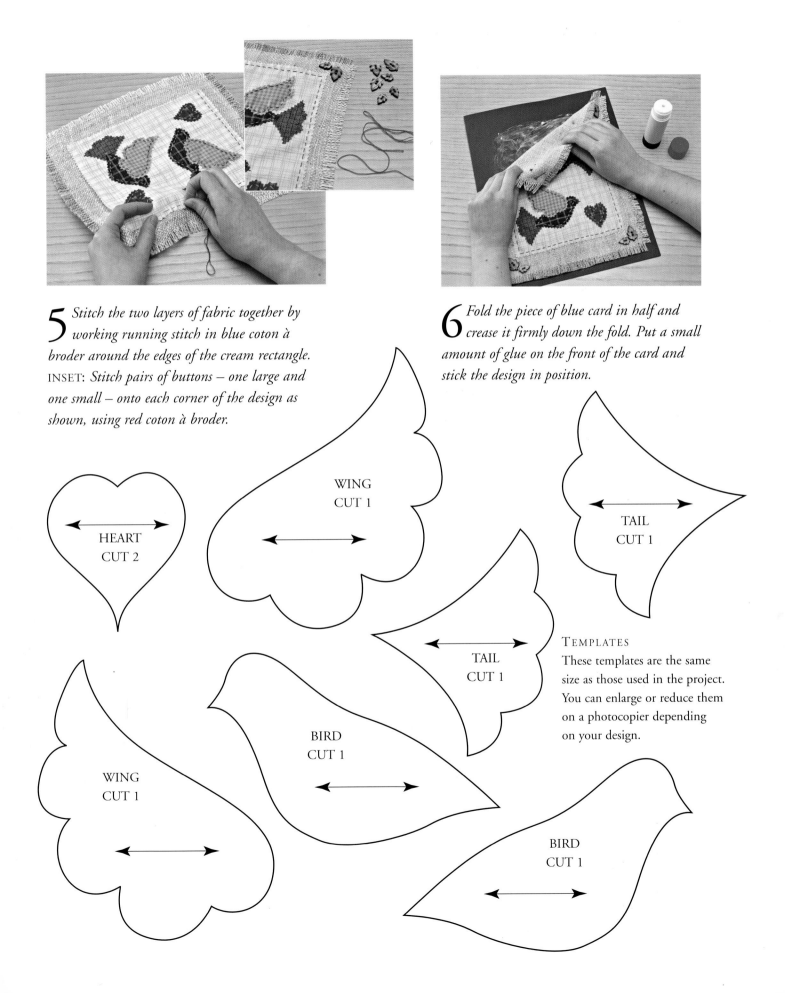

5 *Stitch the two layers of fabric together by working running stitch in blue coton à broder around the edges of the cream rectangle.* INSET: *Stitch pairs of buttons — one large and one small — onto each corner of the design as shown, using red coton à broder.*

6 *Fold the piece of blue card in half and crease it firmly down the fold. Put a small amount of glue on the front of the card and stick the design in position.*

HEART
CUT 2

WING
CUT 1

TAIL
CUT 1

TAIL
CUT 1

TEMPLATES
These templates are the same size as those used in the project. You can enlarge or reduce them on a photocopier depending on your design.

WING
CUT 1

BIRD
CUT 1

BIRD
CUT 1

Knotwork Picture

*A*BEAUTIFUL CELTIC KNOT stitched on ivory silk makes a wedding present that the happy couple will treasure for ever. The design uses Italian or corded quilting to make the pattern stand out against the flat background: the stitched channels are threaded with wool from the back before the picture is mounted. You can use any colour of silk to stitch the knot; work it in colours to suit the recipients' house; or choose a suitable colour-scheme for a silver, gold, emerald, sapphire or ruby wedding anniversary. The design also looks very effective worked in gold or silver metallic thread on an ivory background.

Materials

- *38cm (15in) square of ivory silk*
- *38cm (15in) square of white cotton backing fabric*
- *Two skeins of white stranded embroidery cotton*
- *Water-soluble marking pen*
- *Small ball of cream Aran knitting wool or trapunto wool*
- *40cm (16in) square of adhesive craft board*
- *40cm (16in) square of gold mounting card*
- *13cm (5in) cream cord*
- *Bodkin or large tapestry needle*
- *Strong glue*
- *Small embroidery scissors*

Tip

Don't worry if you can't obtain adhesive board; secure your design with strips of masking tape, and stick the gold card frame in place with glue or double-sided tape.

OPPOSITE: *Italian (corded) quilting creates an intriguing texture on the Celtic knot design by slightly raising the stitched lines. To make the present extra special, you could work the running-stitch outlines in fine gold or silver thread instead of white.*

Making the Knotwork Picture

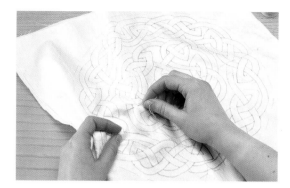

1 Using a photocopier, enlarge the design on page 35 by 200%. Lay the photocopy on a flat surface and pin the square of silk on top, so that there is an even border. Trace the lines of the design carefully using the water-soluble marking pen.

2 Lay the square of backing fabric out flat and position the marked silk, right side up, on top. Stitch a line of basting just outside the circular design, and run a line or two of basting across the design.

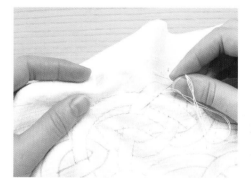

3 Using two strands of white embroidery cotton, stitch small, even running stitches along all the marked lines. The exact length of the stitches doesn't matter: just keep them even in length and in their distance from each other. When all the lines have been stitched, spray or sprinkle the design with cold water to remove the pen marks, and leave it to dry completely. When dry, lay the design face down on a soft surface and press it with a warm iron from the back.

4 On the back of the work, and using small, sharp embroidery scissors, make a tiny slit in the backing fabric at the end of each stitched channel (where the channel stops to go under another one). Be very careful not to slit the silk.

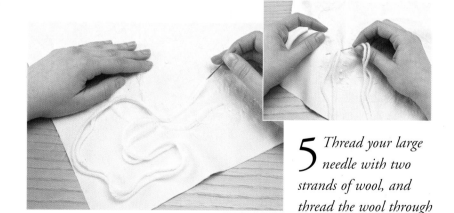

5 Thread your large needle with two strands of wool, and thread the wool through each of the channels. Bring it out where you need to go over a channel, then take it back into the work at the beginning of the next channel.
INSET: When you come to a sharp point in the design, make an extra slit at the point; bring the wool up and then back down through the same slit again, leaving a tiny loop of wool. This creates a definite point rather than a curve on the front of the design.

6 *Trim the square to 35.5cm (14in).*
Make sure there is an even border of
fabric at each edge of the design. Peel the
backing paper off the adhesive board; lay
the design, right side up, in the centre
and press it onto the board.

7 *Cut a 30-cm (12-in) square out of the centre of the gold card*
to leave a frame 5cm (2in) wide. Lay the gold card, face up,
on top of the adhesive square, and press the edges of the card
against the adhesive. INSET: *Cut a 5-cm (2-in) square of gold*
card. Turn the design face down and dab some glue in one corner;
position the cord loop on the glue and cover with the gold square.

TEMPLATE
This template should be
enlarged by 200% to a
diameter of 28.5cm (11^{1}/2in).

Confetti Quilt

A ROMANTIC HEART MADE FROM confetti shapes decorates this double bed quilt, surrounded by ribbon borders. The design looks as though it's stencilled, but is actually created using a clever technique known as shadow quilting; bright fabric shapes are trapped under a layer of softening muslin (US: cheesecloth), and surrounded with decorative stitchery. This design would look equally effective in a limited colour scheme – pinks and greens, for instance, or yellows and blues.

Materials

- *204cm (80in) square, and 214cm (84in) square of white cotton fabric*
- *204cm (80in) square of 2oz polyester wadding (US: batting)*
- *4m (4 yd) of white muslin (US: cheesecloth), at least 122cm (48in) wide*
- *Cotton fabric, plain or with a small print; one fat quarter in purple, turquoise, bright green, mid-green, light green, orange, rich yellow, gold, pink, red, pale blue*
- *1m (1yd) mid-blue cotton fabric*
- *Sewing threads in colours to match the fabrics*
- *4.5m (5yd) double-sided bonding web, at least 46cm (18in) wide*
- *Pencil*
- *Newspaper*
- *Masking tape*
- *Water-soluble or fading pen*

TIP

If there are any pen marks still visible once the braid is stitched in place, dab with a slightly damp cloth to dissolve them.

OPPOSITE: *Scattered confetti shapes create a heart-shaped garland edged by ribbons on this shamelessly romantic double bedspread; stitch it as a wedding present and it will be treasured forever.*

Making the Confetti Quilt

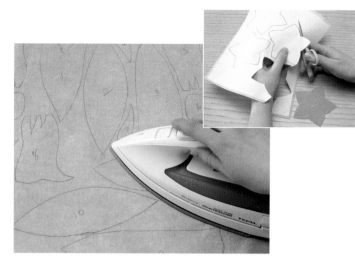

1 *Enlarge the confetti templates on page 41 by 110%. Enlarge the ribbon templates on page 40, onto a 10cm (4in) grid to the appropriate size. Trace the set of ribbon templates four times onto the paper side of the bonding web. Cut nine 30cm (12in) lengths of bonding web and cover each piece with as many tracings as possible of each different confetti template.*

2 *Lay the ribbon tracings, paper side up, on the back of the mid-blue fabric and fuse them into position; then fuse half of the four-petalled flowers onto the remainder of this fabric and the rest onto the pale blue. INSET: Fuse the remainder of the confetti shapes onto fabric of the appropriate colour, following the colours indicated on the templates on page 41, and carefully cut out all the shapes using sharp embroidery scissors.*

3 *Stick several sheets of newspaper together with masking tape to create a sheet at least 115cm (45in) square. Fold this in half, and draw half a heart garland; cut away the excess paper from around and inside the shape.*

4 *Press a fold down the centre of the smaller square of white fabric. Unfold the paper heart and position it on the fabric so that the folds align. Trace around the inside and outside edges of the heart in water-soluble pen.*

5 *Keep back an assortment of about 20 confetti shapes, then peel the backing papers off the remaining shapes. Lay the shapes inside the heart garland design so that they create a pleasing, random pattern. When you are happy with the positioning, fuse them all carefully in place with a warm iron. Press the fold out of the fabric at the same time. Using the water-soluble or fading pen, draw a line 28cm (11in) in from each edge of the fabric square.*

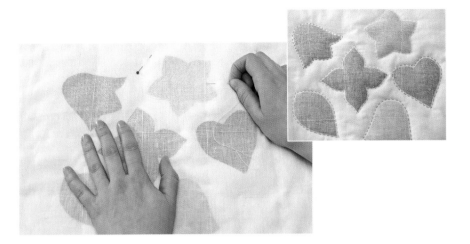

6 *In each long section follow the order of assembly on page 40 to position a set of ribbon shapes, peeling off the backing papers and fusing them as before. In each corner square fuse a scattering of the remaining confetti shapes.*

7 *Lay the larger square of fabric right side down on a flat surface and cover it with the wadding. Lay the decorated square, right side up, on top of the wadding. Cut a 122-cm (48-in) square of muslin and pin it over the heart shape. Stitch a grid of horizontal and vertical basting lines at even intervals across the centre of the quilt. Take a large stitch over each confetti shape.* INSET: *Using matching colour thread for each piece, quilt around each confetti shape with small, even running stitches. When all the outlining is complete, remove the basting threads.*

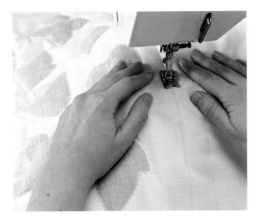

8 *Thread your sewing machine with white thread and set it to a medium-length and medium-width zigzag stitch. Stitch all the way around the heart outlines – internal and external – marked with the water-soluble pen. Cut the excess muslin away from outside the shapes, cutting close to the zigzag line.*

9 *Cut two 204 × 30cm (80 × 12in) rectangles of muslin and pin them over the top and bottom, so that they overlap the straight pen lines slightly. Baste the layers together as before, then quilt around each blue ribbon section with blue sewing thread. When all the stitching is complete, remove the basting threads, then machine-stitch and trim along the pen lines as before. Make an extra line of machine stitching along the pen lines between the corner squares and the ribbon sections. Cut two 152 × 30cm (60 × 12in) rectangles of muslin. Pin and baste these over the ribbon designs at the sides of the quilt, then quilt, machine-stitch and trim these sections as before, making sure that you also stitch down the sides of the rectangles.*

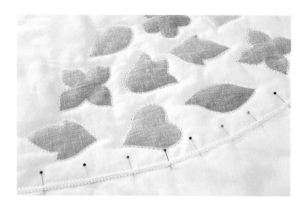

10 *Cut lengths of white braid to fit along the pen lines around the heart. Pin into place then stitch in position with a small zigzag, tucking the raw edges under when they meet around the outline. Stitch four straight lines of braid, from one raw edge of the quilt to the other, to create borders for the ribbons and corner squares.*

11 *Put an embroidery foot on your sewing machine and drop the feed dogs. Beginning around the heart shape and working outwards towards the edges of the quilt, work a large vermicelli pattern to quilt the plain areas, moving the fabric in smooth curves under the machine foot. Fold the edges of the backing fabric over to the front in a double hem, then stitch into place with machine straight stitch.*

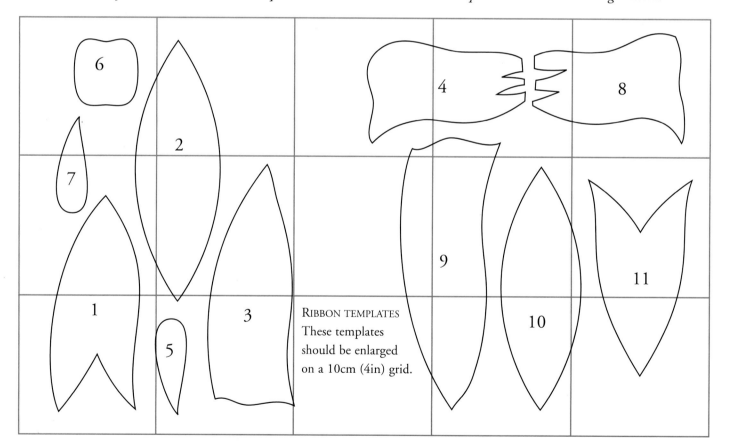

RIBBON TEMPLATES
These templates should be enlarged on a 10cm (4in) grid.

ORDER OF ASSEMBLY
Follow the order shown to position the ribbon pieces before fusing.

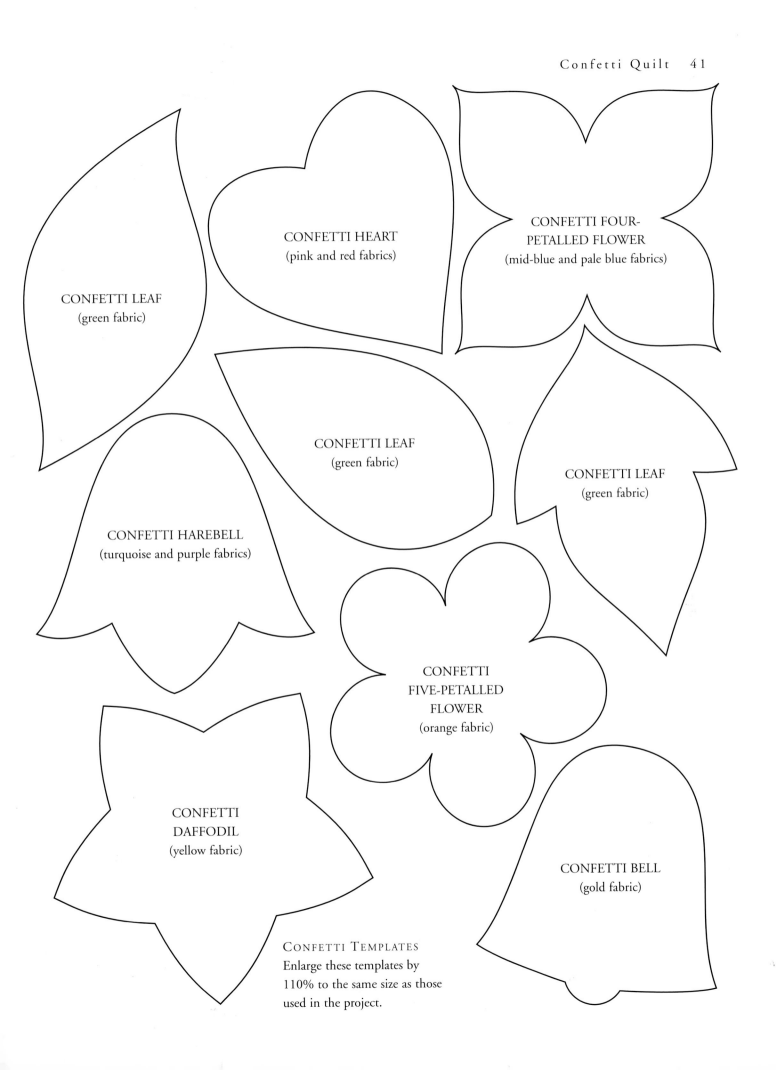

CONFETTI LEAF
(green fabric)

CONFETTI HEART
(pink and red fabrics)

CONFETTI FOUR-
PETALLED FLOWER
(mid-blue and pale blue fabrics)

CONFETTI LEAF
(green fabric)

CONFETTI LEAF
(green fabric)

CONFETTI HAREBELL
(turquoise and purple fabrics)

CONFETTI
FIVE-PETALLED
FLOWER
(orange fabric)

CONFETTI
DAFFODIL
(yellow fabric)

CONFETTI BELL
(gold fabric)

CONFETTI TEMPLATES
Enlarge these templates by
110% to the same size as those
used in the project.

ANNIVERSARIES

Make it a day to remember for an anniversary couple, whether they're celebrating their cotton (1st) anniversary, or their diamond (60th). The ideas in this section can be adapted to suit the theme of any anniversary; just check out your scrap basket and see what exotic bits and pieces you've got tucked away which might be just right.

PROJECTS:

Golden Wedding Album
Technique: *foundation piecing*

Silver Wedding Frame
Technique: *machine appliqué*

Hearts Box
Technique: *machine appliqué*

Anniversary Cards
Techniques: *machine appliqué, simple trapunto, hand stitching*

Golden Wedding Album

CELEBRATE FIFTY GOLDEN YEARS in style with a special photograph album to recall the day. Fill the album with keepsakes from the couple's past, beginning with an original wedding photograph. The panel on the front cover uses cream and gold fabrics to echo the occasion. However, you could adapt the design for a silver, ruby or pearl wedding by varying the colours, or simply work with textured whites or ivories for a bridal photo album.

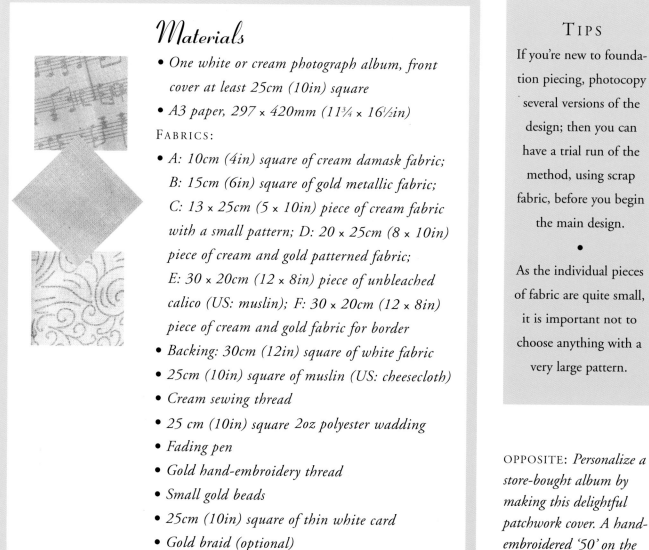

Materials

- One white or cream photograph album, front cover at least 25cm (10in) square
- A3 paper, 297 × 420mm (11¾ × 16½in)

FABRICS:

- A: 10cm (4in) square of cream damask fabric; B: 15cm (6in) square of gold metallic fabric; C: 13 × 25cm (5 × 10in) piece of cream fabric with a small pattern; D: 20 × 25cm (8 × 10in) piece of cream and gold patterned fabric; E: 30 × 20cm (12 × 8in) piece of unbleached calico (US: muslin); F: 30 × 20cm (12 × 8in) piece of cream and gold fabric for border
- Backing: 30cm (12in) square of white fabric
- 25cm (10in) square of muslin (US: cheesecloth)
- Cream sewing thread
- 25 cm (10in) square 2oz polyester wadding
- Fading pen
- Gold hand-embroidery thread
- Small gold beads
- 25cm (10in) square of thin white card
- Gold braid (optional)
- Clear glue

TIPS

If you're new to foundation piecing, photocopy several versions of the design; then you can have a trial run of the method, using scrap fabric, before you begin the main design.

•

As the individual pieces of fabric are quite small, it is important not to choose anything with a very large pattern.

OPPOSITE: *Personalize a store-bought album by making this delightful patchwork cover. A hand-embroidered '50' on the centre provides the perfect finishing touch.*

Making the Golden Wedding Album

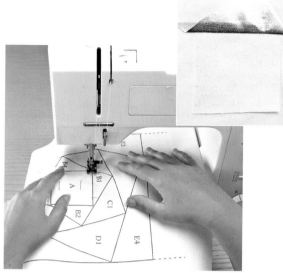

1 *Enlarge the foundation piecing guide on page 48 onto A3 paper. Trace or photocopy templates A–F on pages 48–9, and cut them out. Press all the fabrics. Use the templates to cut out fabric square A and four triangles each for fabrics B–E from the right side of the fabric. Lay the photocopy face down and position fabric square A, right side up, on the reverse side of the photocopy paper, so that the edges of the fabric overlap the central square evenly. Hold the paper up to the light to check the position. Place one of the fabric B triangles on the fabric square, right sides together, so that one long edge aligns with the top edge of the fabric square. Pin in place, at right angles to the raw edge.*

2 *Turn the paper over and stitch along the marked line between the central square and B1, stitching through the paper and both layers of fabric. Start and finish exactly at a marked point.* INSET: *Remove the pins, open out the triangle and press to set the seam.*

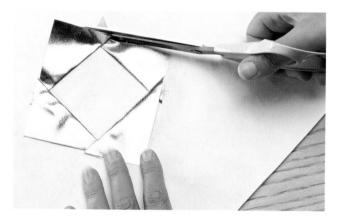

3 *Add the three remaining fabric B triangles in the same way, working around the central square in a clockwise direction. When the square is complete, trim away the points to neaten them.*

4 *Working in the same way add the triangles of fabrics C, D and E. From fabric F, cut two strips 24 × 4cm (9¹/2 × 1¹/2in) and two strips 30 × 4cm (12 × 1¹/2in). Add the short strips to the top and bottom of the design, then add the long strips to the sides, stitching along the top and bottom edges of the large square and along the extended sides of the square.*

5 *Gently remove the backing paper from the wrong side. The stitching creates perforations in the paper, so you should be able to tear the pieces away easily. Press the fabric on the wrong side.*

6 *Use a fading pen to draw the numerals 50 in the central square. Cut the wadding and muslin to the same size as the finished block and baste the three layers together. Hand-quilt around the numerals using gold embroidery thread; stitch gold beads at the corners, then remove the basting thread. Lay the patchwork face down and position the card on the back; glue the edges of the patchwork over to the back of the card. Spread a thin layer of glue all over the back of the card square and stick it to the album front; weigh it down until the glue is dry, then finish off the edges with gold braid secured with a thin line of glue.*

Variation

For a silver wedding anniversary, make up the patchwork block in white and silver fabrics, finishing with a '25' in the centre.

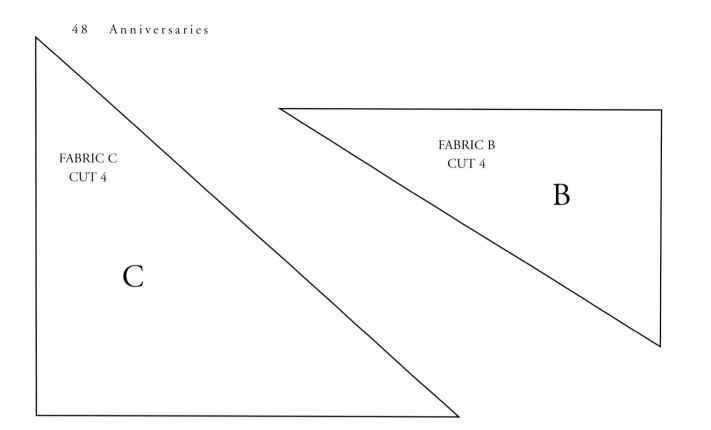

FABRIC C
CUT 4

C

FABRIC B
CUT 4

B

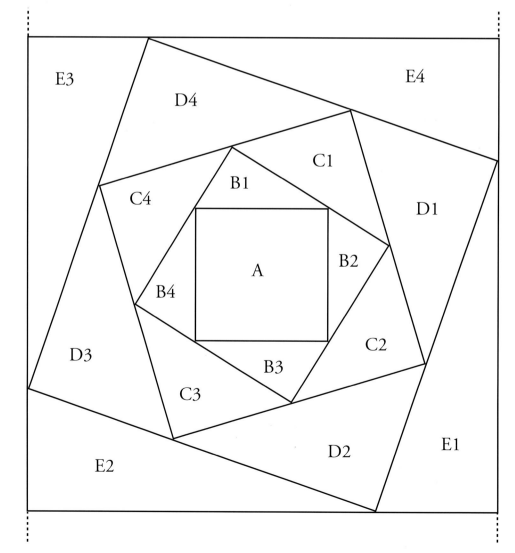

E3

D4

E4

C1

B1

C4

D1

B2

A

B4

C2

B3

D3

C3

D2

E1

E2

FOUNDATION PIECING
GUIDE
This foundation piecing
guide should be enlarged
to A3 size, the edges of the
outer square to measure
just under 23cm (9in).

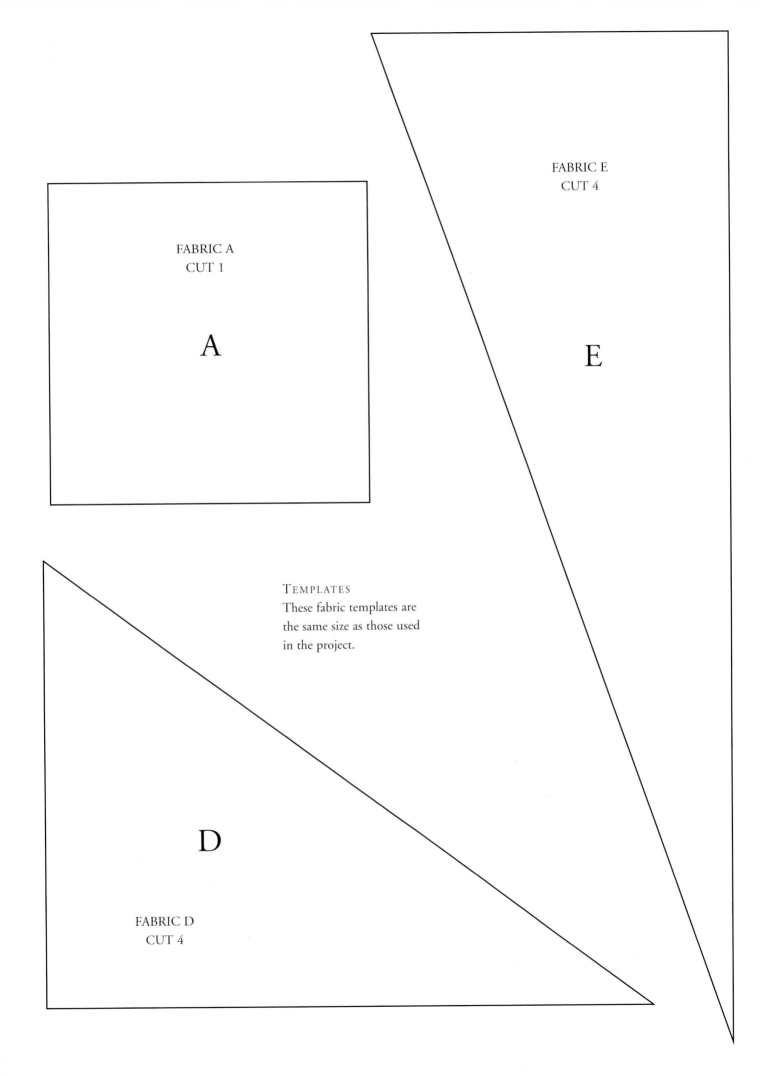

FABRIC A
CUT 1

A

FABRIC E
CUT 4

E

TEMPLATES
These fabric templates are
the same size as those used
in the project.

D

FABRIC D
CUT 4

Silver Wedding Frame

A SILVERY ART NOUVEAU DESIGN appliquéd onto rich blue velvet echoes the effect of Victorian filigree photograph frames. The design looks as though it weaves over and under, but in fact the effect is created by clever machine-stitching on one flat piece of fabric. This colour scheme is perfect for a silver wedding anniversary; try using gold on cream velvet or damask for a golden wedding, or copper on scarlet velvet or silk for a ruby anniversary. This interweaving design would also look very effective worked in wholecloth quilting on a plain background fabric padded with wadding (US: batting); in this case, you wouldn't need to add extra padding to the frame.

Materials

- *36 × 30cm (14 × 12in) piece of dark blue velvet*
- *28 × 33cm (11 × 13in) piece of double-sided bonding web*
- *28 × 33cm (11 × 13in) piece, and 36 × 30cm (14 × 12in) piece of silver or silver-grey fabric*
- *Two pieces thick card, each 32 × 26cm (12^1/$_2$ × 10^1/$_4$in)*
- *1.5m (1^1/$_2$yd) of fine royal blue cord*
- *32 × 26cm (12^1/$_2$ × 10^1/$_4$in) piece of 2oz polyester wadding (US: batting)*
- *Craft knife*
- *Stick glue*
- *Clear glue*
- *Pencil*
- *Silver machine-sewing thread*
- *Masking tape (optional)*

Tips

Some metallic or semi-metallic fabrics are quite sensitive to direct heat. Try out a little piece of yours first, to see whether you need to put a protective layer of fabric or paper between it and the iron. Try to choose a silvery fabric with a bonded backing; this is quite a delicate design, and you don't want the edges to fray.

OPPOSITE: *Create a lasting keepsake with this flowing pattern inspired by Art Nouveau designs. The clever way the stitching is done makes it look as though the fabric weaves in and out, but it's actually very easy to stitch.*

Making the Photograph Frame

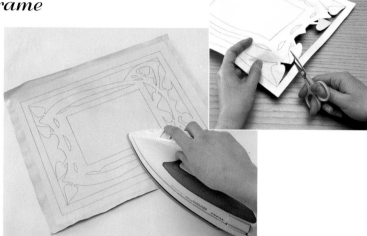

1 Use a photocopier to enlarge the design on page 55 by 130%. Lay the design face up on a flat surface and cover it with the bonding web, paper side up; pin the two layers together or secure them with masking tape to stop them moving. Trace the design onto the paper side of the bonding web.

2 Lay the smaller piece of the silvery fabric right side down on the ironing board and position the bonding web, paper side up, on top; fuse the bonding web into position with a warm iron. INSET: Carefully cut out the design along the marked lines.

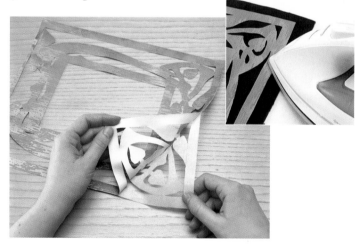

3 Lay the blue velvet, right side up, on your ironing board. Peel away the backing paper from the filigree design and position it carefully on the velvet, leaving an even border of fabric all around the design. Make sure that the outside and inside rectangles are straight and that the corners are at right angles. INSET: When you are happy with the positioning, carefully fuse the design into place with the point of a warm iron, protecting the silver fabric from direct contact with the iron if necessary. Using just the point of the iron on the silvery fabric means that you won't crush the pile of the velvet.

4 Thread your machine with silver thread, and set it to a small zigzag stitch. Beginning with the outside and inside rectangles, stitch around all the edges of the silver fabric, finishing off the thread securely whenever you complete a section. Follow the stitching diagram on page 54 (left) to create the overlapping pattern. Lay the design face down on a towel or other soft surface (again, this is to prevent you from crushing the pile) and press it with a warm iron.

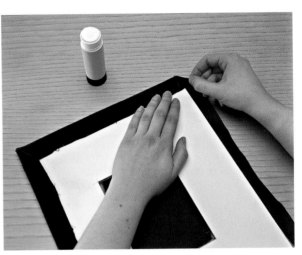

5 On one of the pieces of card, draw a rectangle as shown in the diagram (page 54, right). Use a craft knife to cut away the central rectangle. Cut a similar rectangle out of the centre of the wadding rectangle. INSET: Put a small amount of stick glue onto the card frame and stick the wadding in place; don't use too much glue – just enough to hold the wadding in place.

6 When the glue is completely dry, lay the padded card frame, wadding side down, on the back of your appliqué piece. Spread a little stick glue in the corners and fold down each corner of the blue velvet to stick them as shown. Keep checking on the front of the design to see that you have the corners even; you should be able to see about 5mm (¼in) of velvet beyond the silver appliqué shape.

7 Once you are happy with the corners, spread stick glue down the long sides of the frame and fold the velvet over to secure it; again, keep checking on the front that the edge is straight and even. Finally, glue the top and bottom edges. With the tip of a sharp pair of scissors, make a slit in the velvet in the middle of the central rectangle. Trim this rectangle to 2.5cm (1in) within the central frame, then clip diagonally into the corners, ending the cut just inside the card frame. INSET: Fold these edges to the back and glue them as before, checking on the front that the edges of the velvet are straight and even.

8 *Lay the larger piece of silvery fabric right side down on a flat surface, and position the second piece of card on top, making sure that there is an even border of fabric all the way around. Fold over and glue the corners and then the straight edges with stick glue. Lay the padded frame face down on a flat surface. Spread a generous amount of stick glue around the bottom and side edges; avoid the top edge, as this is where you will insert the photo. Put the piece of backing card on top, card side down. Put the two pieces under heavy books until the glue is dry.*

9 *Slip the photograph into position through the open edge of the frame. Cut a piece of blue cord to go around the frame with 8cm (3in) to spare. Use a cocktail stick or toothpick to spread a tiny amount of clear glue carefully onto the join between the two cardboard pieces, and glue the cord into position around the edges of the frame. At each corner, make a small decorative loop; at the final corner, tuck the raw ends of the cord between the two pieces of card to secure and conceal them.*

Stitch along the lines of the design as shown in this diagram.

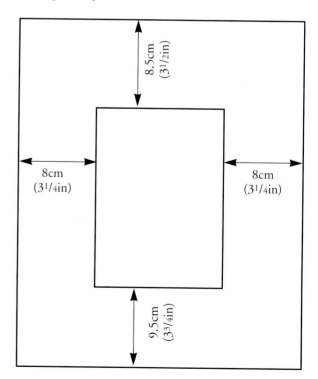

8.5cm (3½in)

8cm (3¼in)

8cm (3¼in)

9.5cm (3¾in)

Cut your card frame to the dimensions shown in this diagram.

TEMPLATE
Enlarge this frame design by
130% on a photocopier.

Hearts Box

ROMANTIC HEARTS IN GOLD and red: a perfect colour scheme for a ruby wedding. Buy or make a simple red square box, then decorate the lid with the appliqué heart design, finished off with red braid. This box would also make a perfect gift for Valentine's Day, filled with delicious chocolates.

Materials

FOR A 14CM (5¹/₂IN) SQUARE BOX

- *18cm (7in) square of cotton fabric (a red and gold hearts print is used here)*
- *13cm (5in) square of gold-print cotton fabric*
- *13cm (5in) square of lightweight double-sided bonding web*
- *Square red leather box*
- *Gold machine thread*
- *14cm (5¹/₂in) square of thin cardboard*
- *14cm (5¹/₂in) square of 2oz polyester wadding (US: batting)*
- *14cm (5¹/₂in) square of Stitch 'n' Tear or other foundation paper*
- *61cm (24in) of red braid*
- *Stick glue*
- *Strong craft glue*
- *Pencil*

TIPS

If you can't get hold of Stitch 'n' Tear (see Materials), use a square of white cartridge paper instead.

•

To make the card stick to the box top firmly, lay a heavy book on top of the lid while the glue dries. The batting will spring back into shape once you remove the book.

OPPOSITE: *The four gold hearts on this design seem just right to celebrate four decades of marriage. Choose a square box covered in fabric or leather, then choose a toning fabric and adapt the design to fit the lid.*

Anniversary Cards

WHETHER IT'S A FIRST WEDDING anniversary or a 75th, make it a day to remember with a romantic card stitched in a suitable colour scheme. You can pick up a theme of a different anniversary in the colours, fabrics and embellishment that you choose; you can really go to town finding little charms and decorations to enhance the theme or to suit the celebrating couple. We've done card or tag designs for cotton, china, gold, ruby, emerald and diamond anniversaries, but you could easily adapt the same idea for the other anniversaries such as silk (12 years), lace (13), crystal (15), silver (25), pearl (30), coral (35) and sapphire (45).

Materials

FOR THE EMERALD WEDDING CARD (55 YEARS):

- *18 x 12.5cm (7 x 5in) piece of emerald green silk dupion*
- *Scraps of cream cotton fabric with a heart design*
- *A4 cream card*
- *Cream sewing cotton*
- *Two gold cherub charms*
- *Small amount of synthetic stuffing*
- *Stick glue*

TIP

Don't stuff the heart shapes too firmly, as this will distort the fabric; you need only a small amount of stuffing to make the design stand out.

OPPOSITE: *This trapunto (padded) card and gift tag have been made to celebrate an emerald wedding anniversary, with two appliquéd love hearts and golden cherubs for embellishments.*

Making the Emerald Anniversary Card

1 Trim the edges of your background fabric rectangle with pinking shears to stop them fraying.

2 Trace or photocopy the heart design on page 63, then use it to cut two hearts out of your scrap fabric. INSET: Pin the hearts in position on your background fabric (the position will depend on which design you are doing, and what else you will be adding to the card).

3 Thread your machine with the appropriate sewing thread and set it to a small zigzag. Stitch around the edges of each heart, beginning and ending at the tip in the centre top.

4 At the back of the work, use small, sharp embroidery scissors to cut a slit in the backing fabric down the centre of each heart shape. Be very careful not to cut your appliqué fabric.

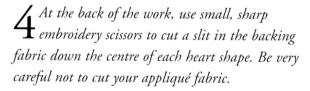

5 Stuff a little of the synthetic stuffing into each heart shape, pushing it into the tip and the curves of the hearts. INSET: Stitch the slits up again with a few large oversewing stitches.

6 *Stitch on any charms, lace or bows to the front of the design. Fold the card in half to create a long card with the fold at the top, and spread some glue over the central panel of the card front.* INSET: *Lay the design onto the card front, making sure that the borders are even all around, and smooth it into place. Leave to dry completely.*

TEMPLATE
This template is the same size as that used in the project.

Variations

Pick out fabrics and trimming appropriate to the anniversary being celebrated, then use the same colour schemes to create matching gift tags. You don't need to stuff these; simply appliqué one heart to a square of the background, then mount the design on a square of card. Punch a hole in the top corner and thread through a loop of ribbon or cord.

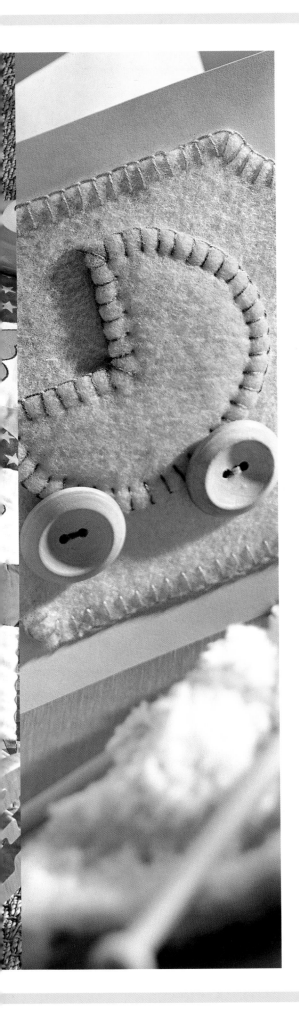

New Baby

So, a baby's on the way – or maybe he or she has already arrived! The proud parents are bound to appreciate a card or little present that has been made specially to greet the new arrival, and you'll find some fun and original ideas in this chapter – from a simple pram or duck design card that can be made in a matter of minutes to a playmat that uses straightforward patchwork and appliqué techniques.

A Ball for Baby

ELEBRATE A BABY'S FIRST birthday by making this brightly coloured ball that is almost guaranteed to become a favourite plaything – the different colours will attract baby's attention, while the ball's soft texture is comfortable for little hands to grasp. The ball is pieced using the 'English' method of patchwork, with backing papers and hand-stitching. Instead of a traditional hexagon template, we have used a pentagon to create the spherical shape. Use 100 per cent cotton fabrics throughout and washable polyester filling, so that the ball can be laundered if necessary. Make sure you stitch the seams securely: even young babies like to chew on their toys!

Materials

- *Scrap paper for backing papers*
- *Twelve 13cm (5in) squares, each of a different cotton fabric, in bright patterns or plain pastel shades*
- *Sewing thread*
- *Basting thread*
- *Polyester stuffing*

TIPS

If the fabric features individual motifs, such as teddy bears or clowns, cut your fabric carefully, so a motif is positioned centrally on a section of the ball.

•

It is easier to remove threads later if you begin basting with a knot on the wrong side of the fabric, finishing off with a single backstitch.

OPPOSITE: *Young babies will love pushing these brightly coloured balls around and crawling after them! Soft to handle, yet tough enough to withstand chewing, they make perfect gifts for a baby's birthday.*

Making the Ball

1 Trace templates A and B on page 69. Cut twelve paper pentagons of template A and one pentagon from each fabric of template B. Pin a paper pentagon A centrally to the wrong side of each fabric shape leaving an even border. Turn the seam allowances over the paper, and baste in place.

2 Join two fabric pentagons, right sides together, by oversewing along one straight edge only, making sure you do not stitch through the backing papers.

3 Join four more pentagons to the sides of the first one, in the same way, to create the flat shape shown far left. Stitch up the side edges between to make a rough hemisphere (shown left). Make up a second hemisphere in the same way. The backing papers keep the shapes rigid.

4 Position the two hemispheres together so that the points of one half fit snugly into the 'V' shapes on the other half. Carefully stitch the two hemispheres together, right sides facing, leaving two adjoining edges open so that the ball can be stuffed.

5 Remove the basting stitches and the papers, then turn the ball right side out. Fold the seam allowances under around the opening and baste. Stuff the shape with the polyester filling.

6 *When the ball is firmly stuffed, stitch the opening closed with ladder stitch and remove the basting thread. Make sure the stitching is secure so that none of the stuffing can be pulled out.*

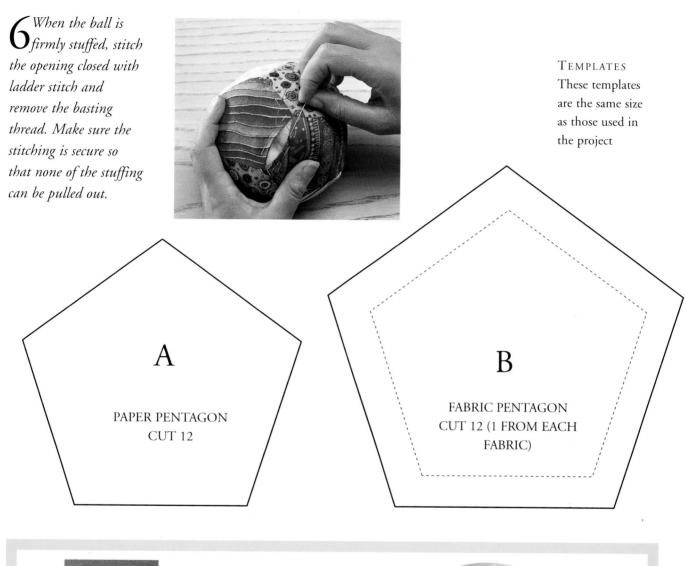

TEMPLATES
These templates are the same size as those used in the project

A

PAPER PENTAGON
CUT 12

B

FABRIC PENTAGON
CUT 12 (1 FROM EACH
FABRIC)

Variation

You can make up a ball in bright or pastel shades to complement a room setting.

We have inserted a bell inside this ball to attract the attention of a young baby.

Pram Quilt

ANY BABY WILL HAVE sweet dreams under this soft creamy-yellow pram quilt. Although it's stitched by hand in the traditional method of wholecloth quilting, it is so small that you'll be able to do it in an evening or two. The finished quilt is beautiful enough to become an heirloom, yet it's practical too; all the materials are hand-washable. After washing, the quilt can be gently tumble-dried or left to dry in the sun so that the quilted design stays fresh and plump.

You can stitch the quilt in traditional blue or pink instead of pale yellow, or try mauve, turquoise, peach or pale aqua. Alternatively, for the real heirloom look, work in white on white or cream on cream.

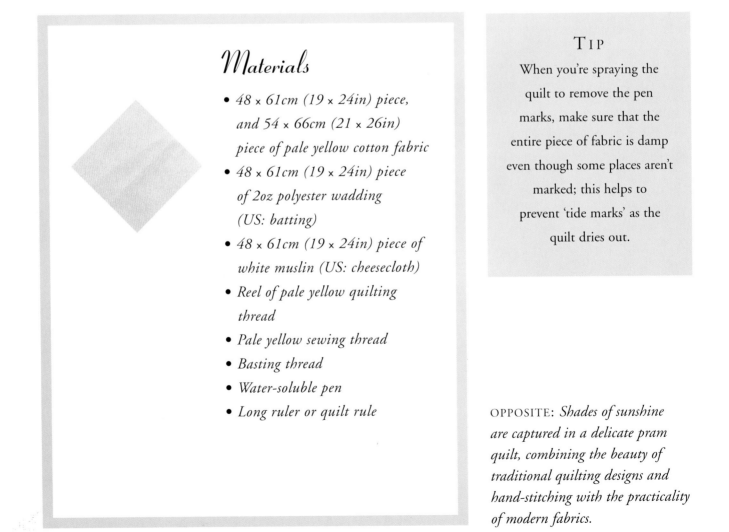

Materials

- *48 x 61cm (19 x 24in) piece, and 54 x 66cm (21 x 26in) piece of pale yellow cotton fabric*
- *48 x 61cm (19 x 24in) piece of 2oz polyester wadding (US: batting)*
- *48 x 61cm (19 x 24in) piece of white muslin (US: cheesecloth)*
- *Reel of pale yellow quilting thread*
- *Pale yellow sewing thread*
- *Basting thread*
- *Water-soluble pen*
- *Long ruler or quilt rule*

TIP

When you're spraying the quilt to remove the pen marks, make sure that the entire piece of fabric is damp even though some places aren't marked; this helps to prevent 'tide marks' as the quilt dries out.

OPPOSITE: *Shades of sunshine are captured in a delicate pram quilt, combining the beauty of traditional quilting designs and hand-stitching with the practicality of modern fabrics.*

Making the Pram Quilt

1 Photocopy the feather design on pages 74–75, enlarging it by 132% to the correct size. Lay the smaller piece of yellow fabric, right side up, over the feather design, ensuring that there is an even border of fabric all around the design. Pin the fabric to the paper to make sure that it doesn't slip, then trace the design using the water-soluble pen.

2 Once the feather design is complete, draw an outline 5mm (1/4in) around the outside and inside edges of the shape. Using the long ruler and the water-soluble pen, draw a straight line 4cm (1 1/2in) in from each edge of the fabric. Then lay the ruler or quilt rule diagonally across the design from one corner of the border to the opposite one, and mark the straight line across the design. Mark parallel lines at 4cm (1 1/2in) intervals until the design is covered. Then lay the ruler diagonally across the design in the other direction, and mark the lines in the same way to create a diamond pattern.

3 Lay the muslin on a flat surface and cover it with the wadding. Lay the marked fabric, right side up, on top of the wadding. INSET: Stitch a grid of horizontal and vertical basting lines at regular intervals to make the quilt 'sandwich'.

4 Beginning at the centre of the design and working outwards, quilt the design in quilting thread using small, even running stitches. Begin with a knot on the back of the work, and finish off each thread securely at the back.

5 *When all the quilting is complete, remove the basting stitches and spray the design lightly with cold water to remove the pen marks; leave to dry completely. Trim away any excess wadding and muslin from the sides of the quilt top to leave a neat, even rectangle.*

6 *Lay the larger backing piece of yellow fabric right side down on a flat surface and position the quilted design, right side up, on top, making sure that there is an even border of fabric all the way around. Fold the excess fabric over to the front of the quilt in a double hem, and pin it into position (inset).*

7 *Slipstitch with sewing thread along the edge of the fold to finish the quilt.*

Variations

Try the same design in a different colour-way; for the quilt below we used a soft purple-blue plain cotton for the front of the quilt and a patterned fabric in a darker shade for the backing and binding piece.

TEMPLATE
Enlarge this feather design
by 132% on a photocopier.

Playmat

A NY NEW BABY – and its parents! – would love this cheery playmat, decorated with simple appliqué shapes. It's a great project for using up all those brightly coloured fabrics from your stash, as anything goes. Just pick a good mixture of colours and tones, and spread them evenly through the design. Follow either the imperial or the metric measurements throughout; they are not exact parallels, but have been calculated to make all the different pieces fit together properly!

Materials

- Large scraps (fat quarters or a bit less) of 16 different bright fabrics, prints and plains
- Nine 17cm (7in) squares of cream cotton fabric (e.g. cheesecloth)
- Twenty-four 17 x 13cm (7 x 5in) strips of fine white or cream cotton fabric
- 102cm (40in) square of brightly coloured backing fabric
- 92cm (36in) square of 2oz polyester wadding (US: batting)
- Sewing threads in 9 different bright colours
- Stranded embroidery threads in bright colours to tone with your fabrics
- Stitch 'n' Tear or white cartridge paper
- Bondaweb or other double-sided bonding web

TIPS

The flip and sew method of strip-piecing is very quick, but to make it even quicker you could create twelve 17 x 26cm (7 x 10in) pieces and then cut each one in half.

•

You'll find that a rotary cutter and board are very useful for cutting all the squares, strips and rectangles.

OPPOSITE: *This project is perfect for using up your scraps of bright plains and cheerful novelty prints. The crazy patchwork used for the sashing pieces is very quick and easy to create, and sets off the simple appliqué squares perfectly.*

Making the Playmat

1 *Cut a 13cm (5in) square from each of the bright fabrics and set aside. Trace or photocopy the three appliqué shapes on pages 80–81, then trace each one three times onto the paper side of the bonding web. Choose nine of the bright fabrics for the appliqué shapes.*

2 *Fuse one shape onto the back of each appliqué fabric with a warm iron, then cut the shapes out along the marked lines.*

3 *Peel the backing paper off the appliqué shapes, and position one in the centre of each square of cream fabric, right side up. Fuse the shapes into position with a warm iron.*

4 *Set your sewing machine to a small, close zigzag, and sew around the edge of each appliqué shape in a contrasting colour. Use Stitch 'n' Tear or cartridge paper underneath the shape to stop it puckering. Tear the paper away when the stitching is complete. For the butterflies, stitch around the outsides of the lower wings first, then the upper wings, extending the line to the body. Stitch a thin body shape, tapering it at both ends.*

5 *Using three strands of embroidery cotton in contrasting colours, stitch simple features onto the teddy shapes using backstitch for the nose and mouth and satin stitch for the eyes. Embroider antennae onto the butterflies, using backstitch ending in French knots, then work a circle of straight stitches onto the centre of each flower shape. Press all the pieces from the back.*

6 *Cut the remaining pieces of bright fabric into random strips of different widths and angles, keeping all the edges straight. (A rotary cutter is useful.) Take one of the rectangles of white or cream fabric and cut a strip of bright fabric to fit one end. Pin this in position, right side up.*

7 *Choose a contrasting strip and pin it face down over the first piece, raw edges aligned. Stitch a small seam along the raw edges.* INSET: *Fold the second piece to the right side, then add a third piece in the same way.*

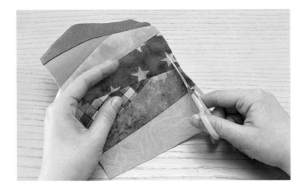

8 *Continue with this 'flip and sew' method, varying the shapes, sizes and angles of the fabric strips, until the foundation piece is covered. Trim away any excess fabric from around the edges so that the piece still measures 17 × 13cm (7 × 5in). Cover all the twenty-four foundation rectangles with strip-piecing in the same way.*

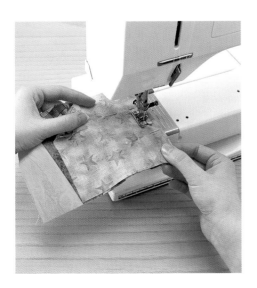

9 *Lay all the pieces out following Diagram 3 on page 80, to form the playmat shape. Adjust the positions of the different squares and rectangles so that you have a good balance of colour and texture across the playmat. Begin piecing the horizontal sashing strips (see Diagram 1, page 80) by adding one of the small squares to the end of a strip-pieced section; take 1cm (1/2in) seams throughout. Press the seam open from the back, then add another bright square at the other end of the rectangle. Continue building up the sashing row so that you have a row of four bright squares alternating with strip-pieced rectangles. Make each of the four horizontal sashing strips in the same way.*

Create the three other rows (Diagram 2, page 80) by alternating four vertical strip-pieced sections with three appliqué squares each time, still taking 1cm (1/2in) seams. Keep referring to the diagram to check that you are piecing the sections in the correct order. Once all the rows are complete, join the rows in order (see Diagram 3) to create the quilt top, matching the seams across the rows. Press the seams open on the back.

10 *Lay the backing fabric, right side down, on a flat surface and position the batting on top, making sure that there is an even border of fabric all the way around. Lay the quilt top, right side up, on top of the batting and secure the three layers with a grid of basting stitches. Quilt the playmat by machine-stitching down the long seams with a wavy line, or around each large and small square by hand if you prefer.*

11 *Fold the backing fabric over to the front of the mat in a double fold to bind the edges; stitch the folded edge down by machine to finish the playmat.*

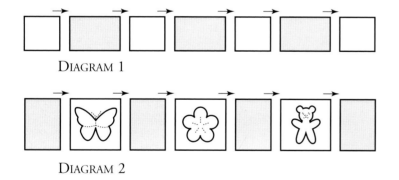

DIAGRAM 1

DIAGRAM 2

Diagram 1: Make four sashing strips.

Diagram 2: Make three rows using appliqué squares

Diagram 3: Assemble the rows in the order shown here to create the playmat.

= strip-pieced sashing block

= coloured square

DIAGRAM 3

TEMPLATES
These templates are the
same size as those used in
the project.

New Baby Card

WELCOME A NEW BABY to the world with this cute card, stitched in a matter of minutes from offcuts of felt or fleece. The soft fabrics, blanket-stitch appliqué and edging, plus the wooden button trim, give the whole design a rustic feel. Blanket stitch is very easy to work; just keep your stitches even in height and work them at even intervals along the edges of the fabric. Don't pull them too tight; the loop of thread should lie snugly against the edge of the fabric.

Materials

FOR THE PRAM DESIGN:

- *13cm (5in) square of pale yellow felt or fleece*
- *10cm (4in) square of bright yellow felt or fleece*
- *Coton à broder, one skein each in turquoise and gold*
- *Two large wooden buttons*
- *30 × 15cm (12 × 6in) piece of pale turquoise card*
- *Stick glue*

TIP
If you need to press the felt pieces, try a test piece first; some felts singe quite easily, so use the coolest iron setting.

OPPOSITE: *A simple outline and two wooden buttons magically create a quaint old-fashioned pram. The design is created using soft fleecy fabrics and appliquéd in blanket stitch to enhance the strong shapes.*

Making the New Baby Card

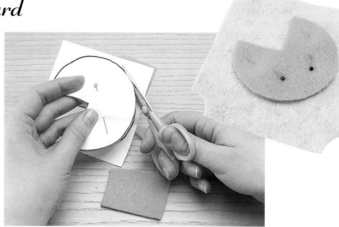

1 *Shape the corners of the pale yellow square by cutting away quarter-circles.*

2 *Trace or photocopy the pram shape on page 85, and use this to cut a shape from the bright yellow fabric.*
INSET: *Pin the pram shape into the centre of the background, making sure that you leave enough room for the wheels.*

3 *Using the turquoise coton à broder, work blanket stitch all around the edges of the pram shape. Make a neat diagonal stitch at the inner corner and each outer corner.*

4 *Use the turquoise coton à broder to stitch the button wheels into position at the base of the pram shape.*

5 *Using the gold coton à broder, work blanket stitch all around the background square, spacing the stitches evenly as you work around the corners.*
INSET: *If the edges of the felt square have become wavy while you've been stitching, lay the design face down on a soft surface (such as a towel) and press gently on the back with a cool iron.*

6 *Fold the card in half to create a square card opening at the right side. Spread a little stick glue over the centre front of the card, then position the pram design so that there is an even border all around and stick it in place.*

Variation

To make the duck card, cut the main duck shape from yellow felt, the puddle from dark blue, the wing from pale orange and the beak from orange. Shape the corners of the background square as for the pram card, and pin the pieces in position on the background square. Work blanket stitch around the outside edges of the appliqué shapes, then finish off the edge of the felt square as for the pram design. Add a bead for the eye. This design will fit the same sized card as that used for the pram.

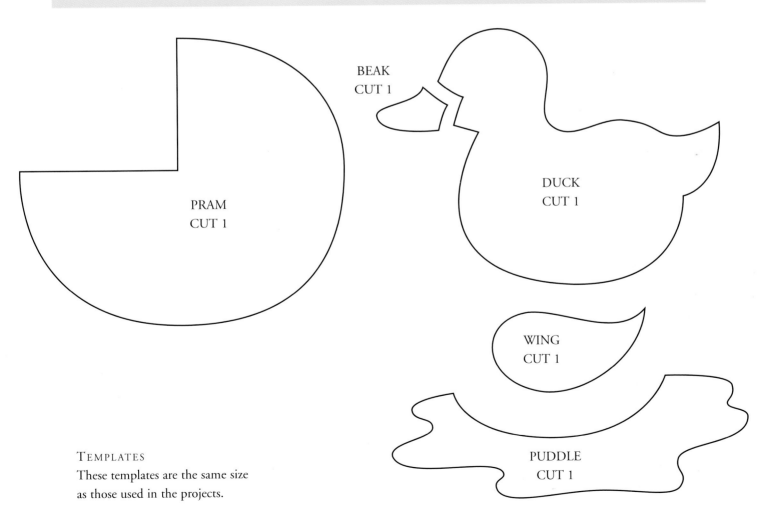

PRAM
CUT 1

BEAK
CUT 1

DUCK
CUT 1

WING
CUT 1

PUDDLE
CUT 1

TEMPLATES
These templates are the same size as those used in the projects.

CHRISTMAS CELEBRATIONS

The festive season is always a great excuse to go to town and decorate the whole house. I hope that these projects will give you some fresh ideas for your Christmas celebrations, from a tree mat decorated with a seasonal wreath to exotic tree decorations; from a traditional stocking to home-made Christmas cards.

PROJECTS:

Tree Decorations
Technique: *hand-sewn patchwork over papers*

Christmas Stocking
Techniques: *machine appliqué, machine sewing*

Christmas Cards
Technique: *hand appliqué*

Christmas Tree Mat
Techniques: *stained glass patchwork, machine sewing*

Tree Decorations

THE RICH FABRICS of these decorations look wonderful against the dark green foliage of Christmas greenery, set off by the gold tassels and beads. Stitch them in exotic purples and jades, or in royal blues, red and greens for a more traditional feel. The assembly of the decorations is very straightforward, based on the English paper-piecing method.

Materials

FOR EACH DECORATION:

- *At least 30cm (12in) square of cotton or silk fabric (if you want to use a particular printed motif in each panel you will need a piece large enough to give you six repeats)*
- *At least 8 x 13cm (3 x 5in) piece of thick card*
- *At least 25cm (10in) square of thinner card*
- *Pencil*
- *Stick glue*
- *Scalpel or craft knife*
- *Steel ruler*
- *Sewing thread to match your fabric*
- *Large gold bell cap*
- *Gold beads, tassel, bell*
- *30cm (12in) gold cord*

TIPS

If the printed design on the fabric isn't quite straight, go with the design rather than the grain.

•

If you want to use a particular repeat motif from a printed fabric, cut the larger template from template plastic, then mark in the seam allowances. Use this to frame each motif accurately before you cut each piece of fabric.

OPPOSITE: *The rich colours of the different fabrics look like jewels suspended from the tree. You could vary the prints to match a particular colour scheme, and even hang the baubles along a mantelpiece to continue the decorative theme.*

Making the Tree Decorations

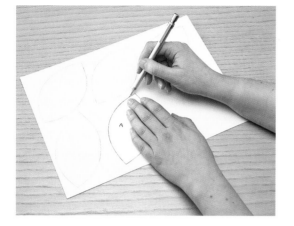

2 Use template A to cut six shapes from the thin card, and template B to cut six fabric pieces.

1 Choose the design you want to create, and trace or photocopy the two relevant templates from pages 92–93; cut the shapes out. Draw around the templates onto thick card and cut them out with a craft knife or scalpel. Template A is for the card shapes; template B is for the fabric.

3 Lay one of the fabric pieces face down and position a card shape on top, making sure there is an even border all the way around. Spread a little glue along the outer edges of the card shape, then fold the fabric over and stick it down. With sharp points, such as the tips of the shapes shown above, fold the fabric down over the point first then stick the other edges over these folds.

4 When all the shapes are covered with fabric, lay the ruler along the centre line of the card and run the tip of a scalpel or craft knife lightly down the line to score it. (Don't press too hard, or you will cut through the card.) INSET: Fold each shape along the centre line, right sides together, to set the folds.

5 *Place two covered shapes wrong sides together, matching motifs if relevant, and oversew them from centre top to centre bottom.*

6 *Continue adding the other shapes in the same way, matching the centre tops and bottoms neatly, until you have only one seam remaining. At the bottom of the decoration, add a 4.5cm (3in) loop of gold cord with a bell or tassel attached, or a string of gold beads in different sizes and shapes; tuck the ends of the cord inside the decoration and stitch them in firmly.*

7 *Cut a 23cm (9in) length of gold cord and fold it in half; pull the looped end through the central hole of the bell cap. Knot the ends near the bottom, and lay the knot inside the top of the decoration. Stitch the final seam, securing the cord with a few stitches when you reach the top.*

Variations

Try the same shapes in Christmassy cotton prints and toning silks, adding beads on the points of some of the decorations.

8 *Pull the bell cap down over the top of the decoration and it's ready to hang.*

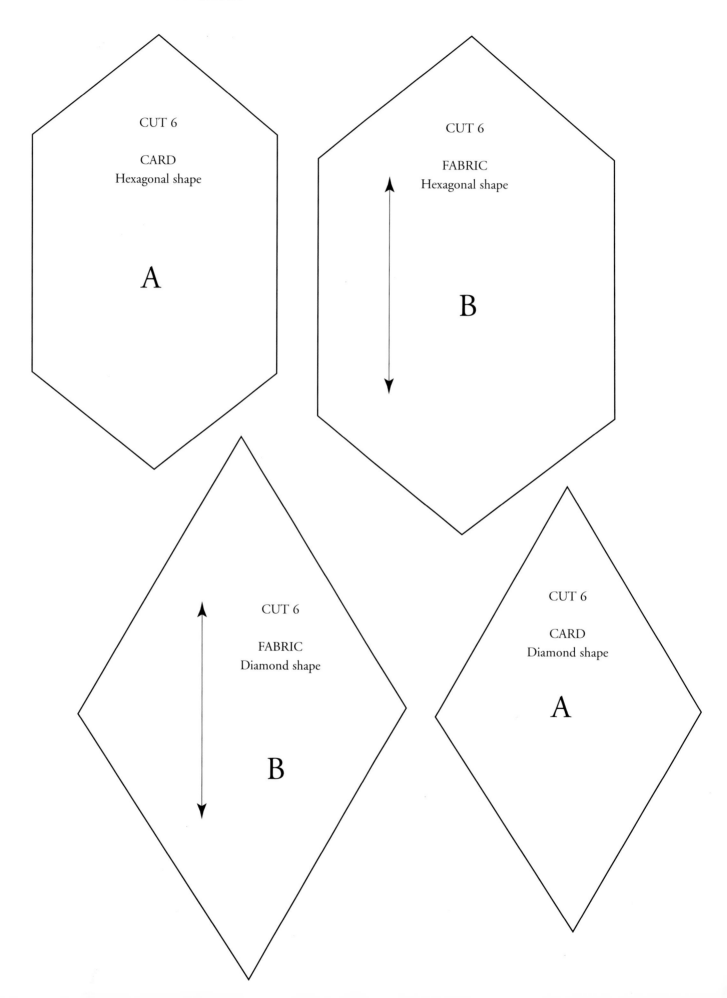

CUT 6

CARD
Hexagonal shape

A

CUT 6

FABRIC
Hexagonal shape

B

CUT 6

FABRIC
Diamond shape

B

CUT 6

CARD
Diamond shape

A

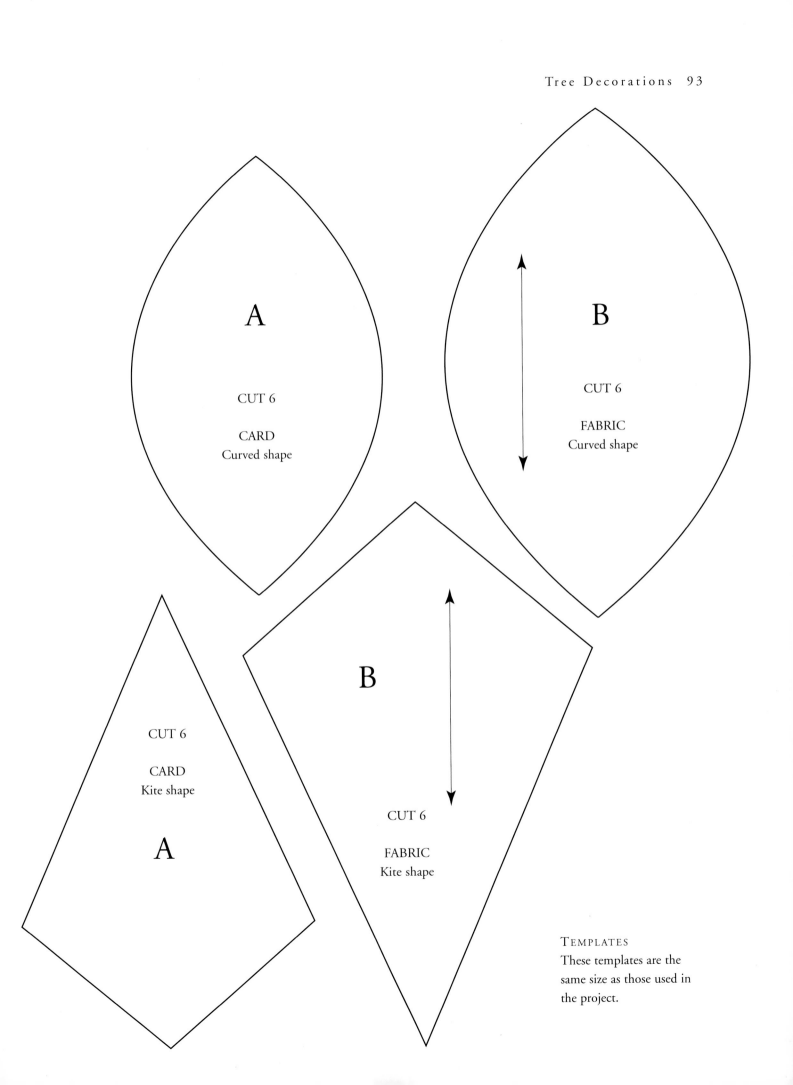

A

CUT 6

CARD
Curved shape

B

CUT 6

FABRIC
Curved shape

CUT 6

CARD
Kite shape

A

B

CUT 6

FABRIC
Kite shape

TEMPLATES
These templates are the
same size as those used in
the project.

Christmas Stocking

DON'T FORGET THE LAST TASK of Christmas Eve – hanging up a large stocking, ready for Father Christmas to fill with goodies! This one has plenty of room for toys and sweets – or you can simply use it as a seasonal decoration if you prefer.

Materials

- *Large scraps, at least 20cm (8in) square, of 14 different cotton fabrics in Christmassy prints and plains*
- *55 × 40cm (22 × 16in) piece of backing fabric in a Christmas print*
- *Two 55 × 40cm (22 × 16in) pieces of green cotton lining fabric, plain or print*
- *59 × 23cm (23 × 9in) piece of green print cotton fabric*
- *Scraps of Christmas ribbons and braids, at least 1m (3yd) in total*
- *2m (2yd) red bias binding, 2.5cm (1in) wide when folded*
- *65cm (25in) red and gold Christmas braid for the top edging*
- *Two 55 × 40cm (22 × 16in) pieces of 2oz polyester wadding (US: batting)*
- *Red and green sewing threads*
- *Gold machine sewing thread*
- *7 large gold beads*
- *Large piece of paper*
- *Pencil*
- *Chalk marker*

TIP

If you want to make the stocking more than once, do two enlargements of the pattern; then you can keep one whole for cutting the stocking shapes, and cut one up for the templates.

OPPOSITE: *Hang this stocking on your mantelpiece or bedhead, and just hope that it's packed full of good things when you wake up the next morning! This is a great project for using up scraps of Christmas-print fabrics and glitzy braids; if you haven't got many, extend them with solid red and green fabrics and pieces of plain ribbon.*

Making the Christmas Stocking

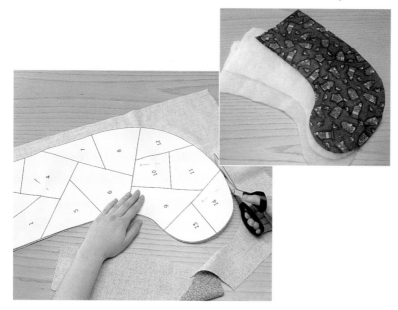

1 *Enlarge the template on page 99 by 196% on a photocopier, or copy it freehand on a large piece of paper to measure 52cm (20½in) high and write in the reference numbers. These numbers will help you to position the pieces later. Lay the two pieces of lining fabric right sides together and use the pattern to cut two stocking shapes.* INSET: *Lay the pattern on the wrong side of the backing fabric and cut out one stocking shape. Use the pattern to cut two stocking shapes from the wadding.*

2 *Cut out piece 1 from the stocking pattern and use it as a template to cut a piece from one of the scrap fabrics, making sure that you position the template on the right side of the fabric. Continue in the same way until you have cut piece 14, making sure that you get a good mix of colours and textures in adjoining fabrics.*

3 *Lay one of the lining pieces right side down on a flat surface and cover with one of the wadding pieces; pin the first piece of fabric in position at the top left of the stocking.* INSET: *Continue pinning the pieces in numerical order (following the reference numbers on page 99).*

4 *When complete, begin cutting pieces of Christmas ribbon and braid to cover the joins between the fabric pieces. Start with all the lines marked A, then B and so on, following the diagram on page 97. Pin in position.*

5 *Using a small zigzag stitch on the machine, stitch down both sides of each piece of ribbon or braid to secure it; this also quilts the design as you stitch. Continue building up the design, adding the pieces of ribbon and braid in alphabetical order (see diagram below), until all the lines are covered.*

6 *Lay the backing right side down and cover with the other pieces of wadding and lining fabric. Lay the stocking front on top, right side up. Beginning at the top, lay the bias binding over the stocking front so that the raw edges are aligned. Pin in position.*

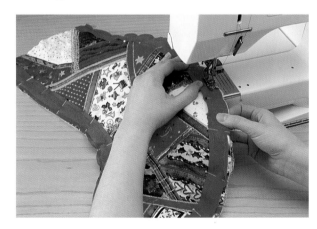

7 *Stitch the bias binding by machine, then turn the folded edge over to the back of the work and stitch it into place by hand or machine.*

ORDER OF STITCHING BRAID
Stitch the pieces of braid in
alphabetical order, A to E,
as shown here.

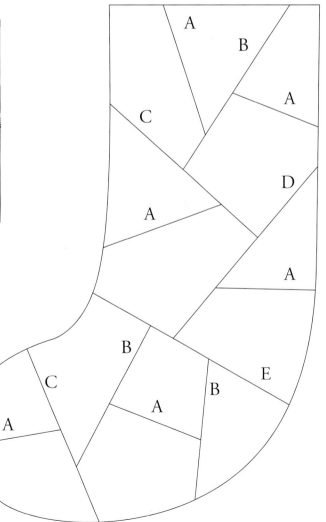

8 *Fold the strip of green fabric in half with the right sides facing, and draw a chalk line 8mm (1/4in) in from the folded edge and from the side edges. Draw another line 4.5cm (1 3/4in) in from the folded edge. Use the chalk to draw a regular zigzag between the lines, beginning and ending at the bottom outside corners.*

9 *Machine stitch down the chalk line at the sides and along the zigzag line. Trim the fabric along the zigzag, clipping across the points and into the top angles.* INSET: *Turn the strip right side out and pull the points out with a pin and press.*

10 *Run two gathering threads along the raw edges, then pull the frill up evenly to fit the top of the stocking.*

11 *Beginning at the centre back, pin the frill inside the top of the stocking, raw edges aligned, then stitch a 1cm (1/2in) seam. Fold the frill over to the right side of the stocking and press.*

12 *Stitch the red and gold braid around the stocking top, making an extra hanging loop at the right-hand side. Finally, stitch a large gold bead to each point on the frill.*

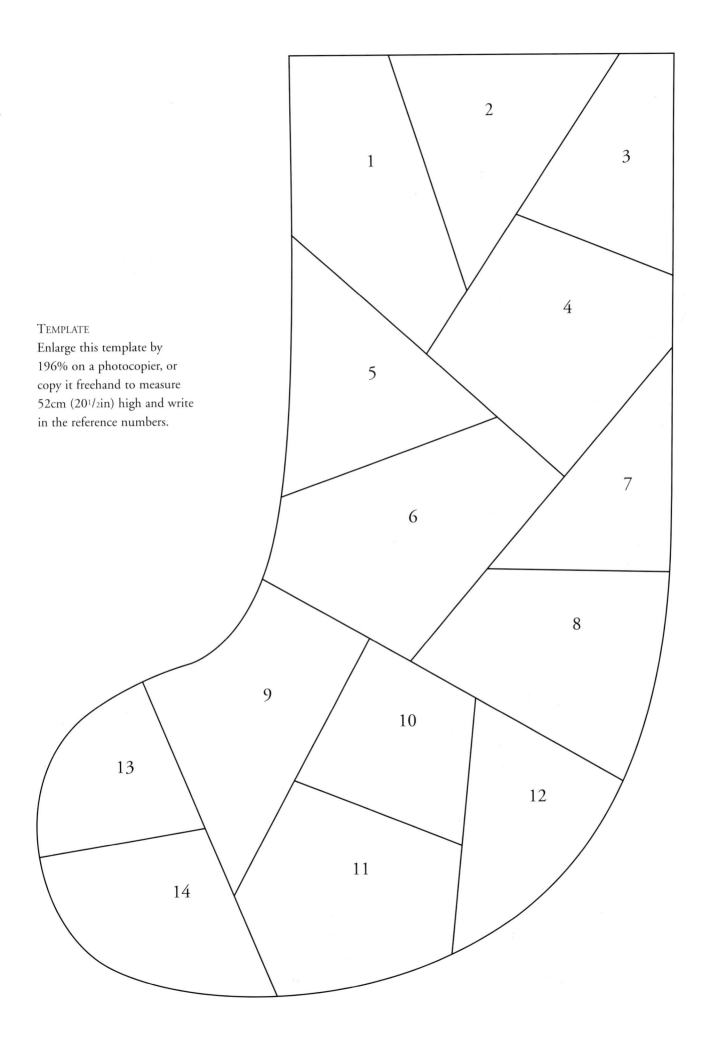

TEMPLATE
Enlarge this template by
196% on a photocopier, or
copy it freehand to measure
52cm (20^1/$_2$in) high and write
in the reference numbers.

Christmas Cards

*T*HERE'S SOMETHING EXTRA SPECIAL about handmade Christmas cards, and these are no exception. Although they're made from scraps of fabric, the strong shapes and bold stitching create striking designs, enhanced with beads and sequins. And the cards are so quick to make that you could produce several different designs in an evening! Use scraps of Christmassy prints and glittery metallics to create the star card and the variations on page 103. You could also try other simple shapes such as a snowman, a set of baubles, a candle or a Christmas wreath.

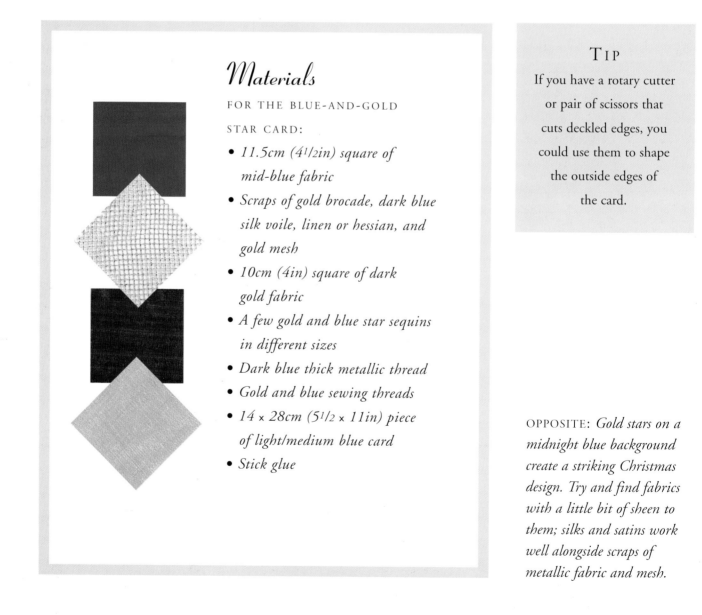

Materials

FOR THE BLUE-AND-GOLD
STAR CARD:

- *11.5cm (4¹/2in) square of mid-blue fabric*
- *Scraps of gold brocade, dark blue silk voile, linen or hessian, and gold mesh*
- *10cm (4in) square of dark gold fabric*
- *A few gold and blue star sequins in different sizes*
- *Dark blue thick metallic thread*
- *Gold and blue sewing threads*
- *14 × 28cm (5¹/2 × 11in) piece of light/medium blue card*
- *Stick glue*

TIP
If you have a rotary cutter or pair of scissors that cuts deckled edges, you could use them to shape the outside edges of the card.

OPPOSITE: *Gold stars on a midnight blue background create a striking Christmas design. Try and find fabrics with a little bit of sheen to them; silks and satins work well alongside scraps of metallic fabric and mesh.*

Making the Star Christmas Card

1 *Trace or photocopy the star shape on page 103. Use this drawing as a pattern piece to cut a rough-edged star out of the dark gold fabric. The edges of these designs are supposed to be uneven, so move the scissors from side to side slightly as you cut the edges of the star shape. Using the same technique, cut the mid-blue backing fabric down to roughly 10cm (4in) square.*

2 *Cut rough-edged rectangles of different sizes from the three remaining fabrics. Pin the first rectangle in position on the backing square.* INSET: *Add the rectangle of gold mesh, overlapping the two slightly. Add the third rectangle to overlap the first two slightly.*

3 *Pin the gold star roughly in the centre of the design; if necessary, adjust the positions of the different pieces at this stage to make a pleasing layout.*

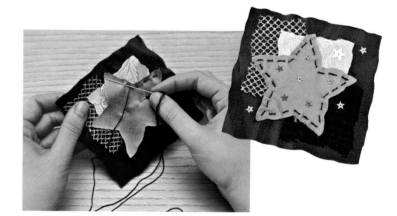

4 *Using the blue metallic thread in a large needle, stitch long, even running stitches near the edge of the star to appliqué it.* INSET: *Using the blue thread, stitch several blue sequin stars onto the gold star. Using gold thread, stitch several gold stars on the rest of the design. If necessary, catch down the backing rectangles with a tiny stitch or two in a matching thread.*

5 *Fold the piece of card in half to make a square. Spread a small amount of stick glue onto the centre of the card front.* INSET: *Stick the finished design in position.*

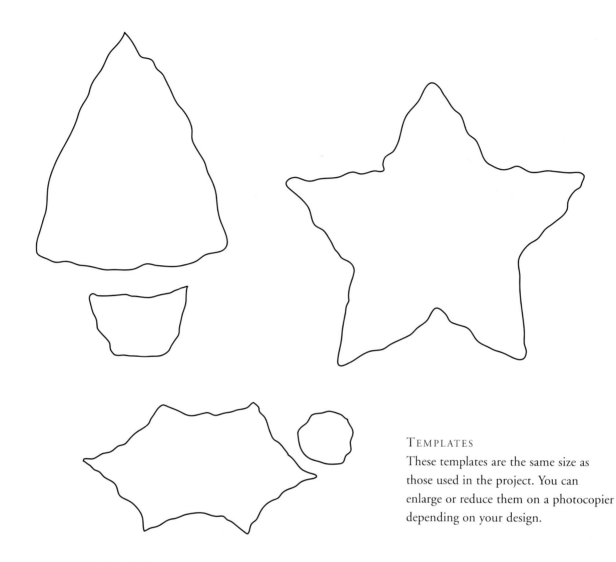

TEMPLATES
These templates are the same size as those used in the project. You can enlarge or reduce them on a photocopier depending on your design.

Variations

The Christmas tree and holly cards are made in exactly the same way, using the templates shown above. Note that the Christmas tree motif has only two, rather than three, rectangles behind it; for this design, cut the rectangles slightly larger than for the other two designs.

Christmas Tree Mat

WELCOMING CHRISTMAS WREATHS are a traditional part of Christmas decorations. Instead of putting one on your door, here's a slightly different idea: create a fabric wreath of holly, Christmas roses, fruit and ribbon, and use it to decorate a cloth mat to go under your Christmas tree.

Materials

- 112cm (44in) square of slightly patterned or textured red fabric

COTTON FABRICS IN THE FOLLOWING QUANTITIES:

- fat quarter of dark green and gold print (for the holly leaves); fat quarter of mid-green mottled print (for the other leaves); fat quarter of red and gold print (for the fruit); fat quarter of cream and gold print (for the flowers); 50cm (1/2yd) white fabric with small Christmassy print (for the ribbon); large scrap of gold print (for the flower centres); large scrap of Florentine-type print (for the inside and tips of the bow)
- 25m (25yd) black bias binding, 12mm (1/2in) wide when folded
- 8m (8yd) Christmassy ribbon, either plain or patterned
- Black and green sewing threads
- Pack of dressmakers' tracing paper
- Chalk marker
- Pencil

TIPS

To save neatening the edges, buy a square Christmas tablecloth in a small print and create the wreath design on top.

•

Use the chalk marker to number the different patches as you cut them to avoid confusion when you come to laying them

OPPOSITE: *As well as setting off your tree and decorations perfectly, this dramatic tree mat serves a practical purpose: it catches all the stray needles that real trees always shed!*

Making the Christmas Tree Mat

1 On one sheet of the tracing paper, create a grid of 15cm (6in) squares. You will need six squares in each direction. Copy the pattern on page 109 onto the squares, so that the design is enlarged as you go. Mark on all the numbers as shown on the pattern to help you group the shapes and assemble the final design.

2 Cut around the inside and outside edges of the wreath. Press the red fabric and lay it on a flat surface, right side up, and position the wreath design on top so that there is an even border at the top and sides. Draw roughly around the inside and outside edges of the design with a chalk marker; this will help you to position the pattern pieces when you've cut them out.

3 Now cut the paper design into its separate pieces (see page 109), and use the pieces as templates. INSET: Pin the templates, right side up, onto the right side of the corresponding fabric, and cut around each piece carefully, cutting slightly outside the marked line.

4 Lay the red fabric out on a flat surface and lay all the patches in place inside the chalk marks. Begin with the bow and work your way around the wreath. Pin all the patches in position securely. INSET: Use the chalk marker to draw in curved lines on all the leaf patches.

5 *Beginning with all the emboldened lines marked in stage A on the diagram (e.g. the midlines down the leaves), cut and pin lengths of bias binding, curving them to fit the marked lines.* INSET: *Set your machine to a small zigzag and thread it with black thread. Stitch these first lines of bias binding in position by making a small zigzag down each side of the bias binding – you don't need to stitch down the raw ends, as these will be covered by later lines of bias binding. Once you have added each sequence of lines, press them carefully.*

stage A

stage B

stage C

stage D

stage E

stage F

stage G

stage H

ORDER OF STITCHING THE BIAS BINDING
Add the bias binding as shown by the emboldened lines from stage A to stage H.

6 *Continue to build up the design by adding lines in the sequence shown on page 107. Fold the binding crisply at the points of the leaves and the joins of the flower petals. To help ease the binding around curves, such as the fruit shapes, press it with a steam iron to loosen the fibres and set the curve before you pin it into place. When two ends of the binding meet, such as when you complete a flower outline, cut the raw ends slightly longer and tuck them under before you stitch.*

7 *The last lines to be added are around the flower centres (stage H). These curves are very tight, so the binding needs some extra help to curve smoothly. Cut a piece of bias binding about 60cm (24in) long, and run a gathering thread down one fold – you can either do this by hand, or use a very long machine stitch. Pull up the gathering thread evenly.* INSET: *You can then ease the binding around the flower centres very easily and stitch it in the usual way.*

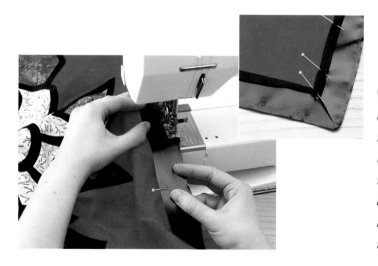

8 *Press under a small hem around each edge of the cloth, and pin the ribbon in place so that it just covers the fold. Stitch a line of zigzag in green down the outside edge of the ribbon.* INSET: *Pin a line of bias binding over the inner edge of the ribbon all round, and stitch it in place by machining down each side as before. If there are any chalk marks left showing on the cloth, simply remove them by rubbing them gently with another piece of cloth.*

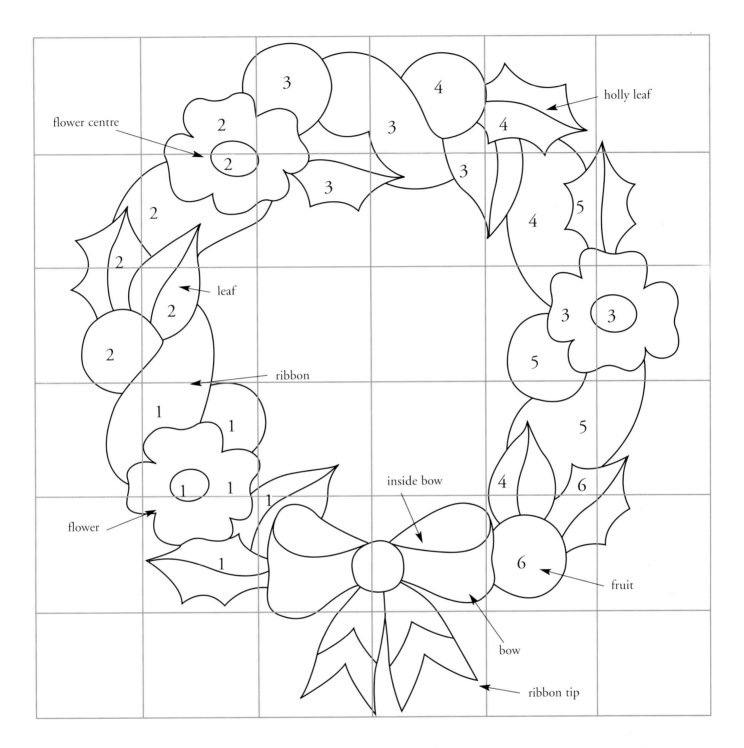

• Cut six holly leaves from the green and gold fabric.

• Cut four ordinary leaves from the mottled green fabric.

• Cut six fruit shapes from the red and gold print.

• Cut three flowers from the cream and gold print (you don't need to cut out the centres of the flowers; these will be covered by the gold patches).

• Cut five ribbon sections and the main pieces of the bow from the Christmassy print.

• Cut the two ribbon tips and the insides of the bow from the Florentine print.

• Cut three flower centres from the gold print.

TEMPLATE
Copy this design onto a 6 x 6 grid of 15cm (6in) squares, enlarging it as you draw. Mark on all the numbers to help you group the shapes.

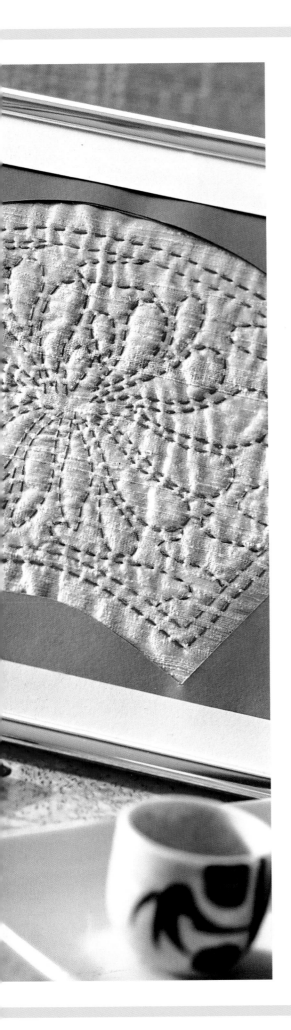

WELCOMES AND FAREWELLS

New home, new job, new country. A long holiday, setting off to college, taking retirement – our lives are marked by all kinds of new beginnings, each one bringing exciting possibilities. This section contains a sample of projects that you can adapt for different occasions.

PROJECTS:

Bon Voyage Picture
Techniques: *machine patchwork, hand quilting*

New Home Cushion
Techniques: *machine patchwork, machine sewing*

Retirement Card
Technique: *sashiko quilting*

Bon Voyage Picture

*W*HEN A FRIEND OR RELATIVE is going on a special journey, wish them 'bon voyage' with this delightful folk-art sailboat. The design is a variation on a classic patchwork block known as sawtooth, and can be stitched by hand or by machine. Choose marbled fabrics or small all-over prints to give a little texture to the scene, and finish with simple quilting for added definition. To make the design into a card, simply reduce the templates on a photocopier, leave the patchwork unquilted, and frame in a ready-made rectangular card mount.

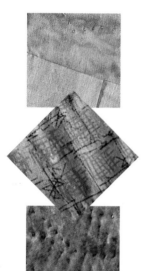

Materials

FABRICS:

- *One pale wood photograph or picture frame, internal aperture 23 × 18cm (9 × 7in)*
- *8 × 15cm (3 × 6in) piece of yellow fabric*
- *23cm (9in) square of mid-blue fabric*
- *23 × 8cm (9 × 3in) piece of mid-brown fabric with a small pattern*
- *23 × 10cm (9 × 4in) piece of green fabric*
- *Piece of pale yellow mounting board to fit your frame*
- *25 × 20cm (10 × 8in) 2oz polyester wadding (US: batting)*
- *25 × 20cm (10 × 8in) piece of white muslin (US: cheesecloth)*
- *Blue sewing thread*
- *Quilting threads to match your fabrics*
- *Narrow double-sided adhesive tape*

TIPS

The accuracy of the seams is vital for successful patchwork; stitch some trial pieces first to make sure that your seams are the correct width.

•

To help match the corners of the yellow triangles when you're completing Step 2, match the patches at the centre seams and then pin, rather than aligning them from the raw edges of the rectangles.

OPPOSITE: *Long after the voyage is over this simple sailboat picture will be a permanent reminder of a special journey.*

Making the Bon Voyage Picture

1 Trace or photocopy the templates on page 115 and cut them out. Use template A to cut four triangles from the yellow sail fabric and six triangles from the blue sky fabric. Use template B to cut one piece from the sky fabric, and template E to cut two pieces. Use template C to cut one piece from the brown boat fabric. Use template D to cut one piece from the green water fabric. Place one triangle (A) of blue fabric and one of yellow fabric right sides together and stitch a seam along the long side. Press the seam open to create a square patch and trim the excess fabric from the ends of the seam. Make four patches in this way.

2 Join two of these patches to make a sawtooth pattern as shown. Join the other two in the same way and press the seams open. Stitch the two rectangles together to form a square containing four yellow 'sails' with four patches of bright blue sky.

3 Add the two short rectangles of sky fabric (E) to the sides of the sail section, making sure you stitch them to the correct sides. Press open the seams and trim the excess fabric.

4 Stitch the remaining two blue triangles to the diagonal edges of the boat base (C) to form the rest of the sky. Press open the seams and trim the points.

5 Stitch the long blue rectangle (B) to the top of the sail design, and the boat section to the bottom of the sail design. Then add the rectangle of green fabric (D) underneath the boat.

6 Cut the muslin and wadding to the same size as the patchwork. Sandwich together and baste through all layers. Outline quilt the sails and boat base in matching thread. Trim away any excess wadding and muslin. Cut a mount and use double-sided adhesive tape on the back to fit the patchwork evenly inside the aperture. Follow the manufacturer's instructions to mount the design in the frame.

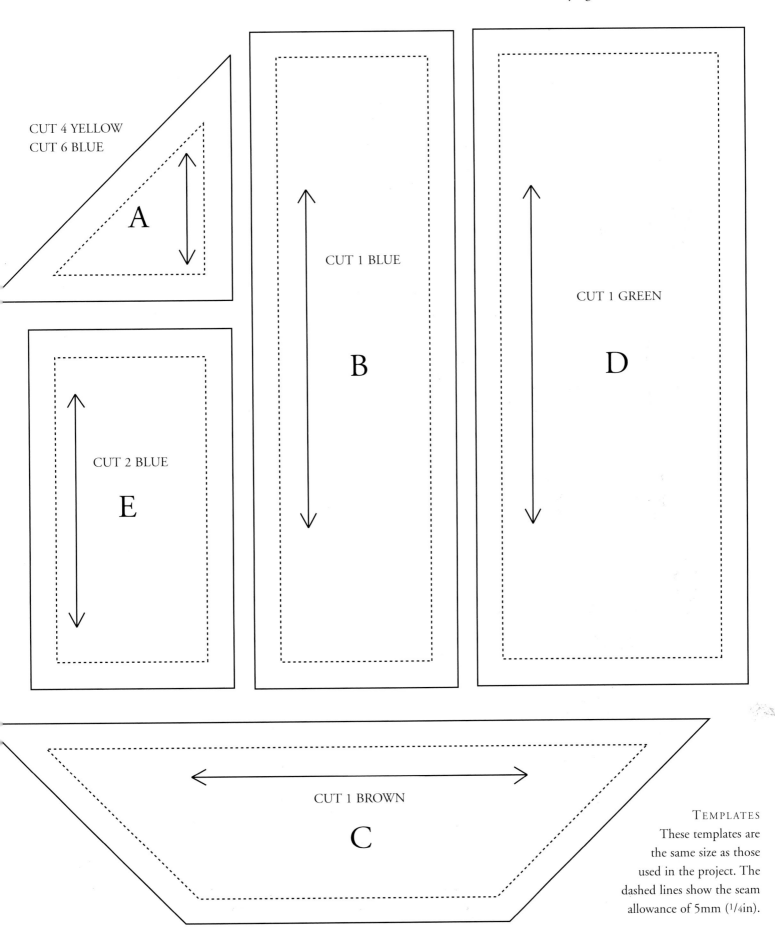

CUT 4 YELLOW
CUT 6 BLUE

A

CUT 1 BLUE

B

CUT 1 GREEN

D

CUT 2 BLUE

E

CUT 1 BROWN

C

TEMPLATES
These templates are
the same size as those
used in the project. The
dashed lines show the seam
allowance of 5mm (1/4in).

New Home Cushion

WHAT BETTER WAY to make a friend feel at home after a house move; it'll be easy to settle in with this cheery cushion cover, based on the traditional American schoolhouse block. If you want to keep the traditional feel, choose soft plaids and tiny prints – or make the design in jazzy bright colours if the home is contemporary. There are many different ways of creating this design; I've chosen one based on a nine-patch block, with a border in a contrasting colour.

Materials

COTTON FABRICS IN THE FOLLOWING COLOURS AND QUANTITIES:

- *40 × 25cm (15 × 10in) piece of soft yellow for the sky*
- *40 × 12cm (15 × 5in) piece of red for the roof and chimney*
- *65 × 25cm (25 × 10in) piece of ochre print for the house*
- *15cm (6in) square of light brown plaid for the door*
- *15cm (6in) square of light red plaid for the windows*
- *40 × 8cm (15 × 3in) piece of dark brown plaid for the ground*
- *50cm (1/2yd) piece, at least 102cm (40in) wide, of soft green plaid for the border and backing*
- *Toning sewing thread*
- *Cushion pad, 46cm (18in) square*

TIP

If you wish, you could quilt the design by hand or machine before you make up the cushion cover. After Step 8, cut a matching square of 2oz wadding and one of muslin and baste the three layers together; quilt around the patches by hand or machine, in toning or contrasting threads.

OPPOSITE: *The traditional little building on this cushion-cover looks just like the schoolhouses of the Amish people, who often use this block design in their quilts. Choose folksy plaids and small prints to enhance the folk-art feel of the design.*

Making the New Home Cushion

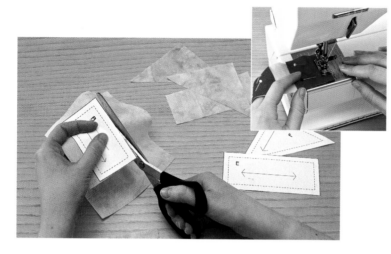

1 *Using a photocopier, enlarge the templates on pages 120–1 by 133%, then use these to cut the pieces listed on pages 120–1. Make sure that you always position the template on the right side of the fabric; this is particularly important for the roof piece.* INSET: *Take the longer strip of sky fabric (E) and position one of the red chimney squares (A) at one end, right sides together, aligning the raw edges. Stitch the seam by hand or machine, taking 8mm (¹⁄₄in) seams throughout; press each seam open after it has been stitched.*

2 *Add the second chimney piece to the other end of the strip in the same way and press the seam open.* INSET: *Add the shorter sky pieces (B) to the ends of the chimney squares to complete the row; keep referring to the diagram on page 119 to check that you are joining the correct pieces.*

3 *Take the large roof piece (H) and pin one of the sky triangles (F) to the right-hand edge, right sides together. Add the triangle of house fabric (G) to the other end of the roof; stitch and press the diagonal seams. Then add the final triangle of sky (F) to the house section to complete the row. Check the length of this row against the chimney section; if either is too large or too small, adjust the seams slightly.*

4 *Pin the short rectangle of house fabric (B) to the top of the door section (D).* INSET: *Stitch and press the seam.*

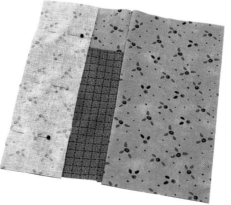

5 *Stitch the large section of house fabric (I) to the right side of the door panel, then add one of the long thin strips (C) to the left side of the door.*

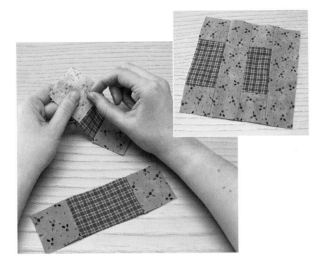

6 *Add a square of house fabric (A) to each end of one window section (B), then press the seams open; do the same with the second window section.* INSET: *Join one long strip of house fabric (C) to the right side of each window section, then join these two sections together.*

7 *Join the door section to the left of the window section to complete the row. Cut a strip of sky fabric 36 × 8cm (14 × 3in), and a matching strip of ground fabric. Follow the diagram (below left) to assemble the rows, adding the sky strip to the top of the design and the ground strip to the bottom (inset).*

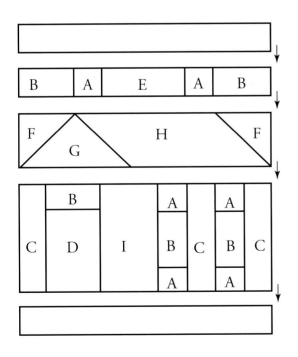

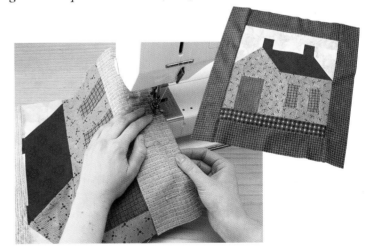

8 *Cut two pieces of green plaid, 51 × 30cm (20 × 12in). From the remaining plaid cut two strips 36 × 8cm (14 × 3in), and two 51 × 8cm (20 × 3in). Add the shorter strips to the top and bottom of the cushion design.* INSET: *Then add the longer strips down the sides to complete the panel.*

ORDER OF ASSEMBLY
Refer to this diagram when you are assembling the separate pieces then join the strips together to complete the schoolhouse block.

9 *To make the back of the cushion, fold under a small double seam on one long edge of each plaid rectangle, and stitch by machine.*

10 *Lay the patchwork panel, right side up, on a flat surface and lay the two green plaid rectangles on top, right sides down, so that they overlap and the raw edges align. Pin together. Stitch a 1.5cm (¹/₂in) seam around the edges. Trim the seams and clip the corners, turn the cover right side out and press, then insert the cushion pad.*

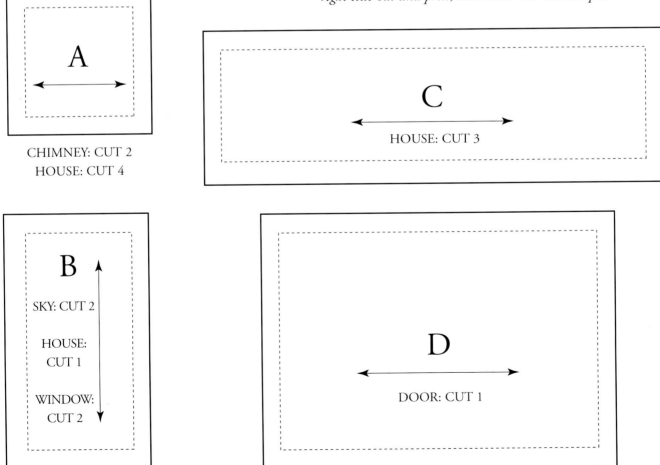

A

CHIMNEY: CUT 2
HOUSE: CUT 4

C

HOUSE: CUT 3

B

SKY: CUT 2

HOUSE:
CUT 1

WINDOW:
CUT 2

D

DOOR: CUT 1

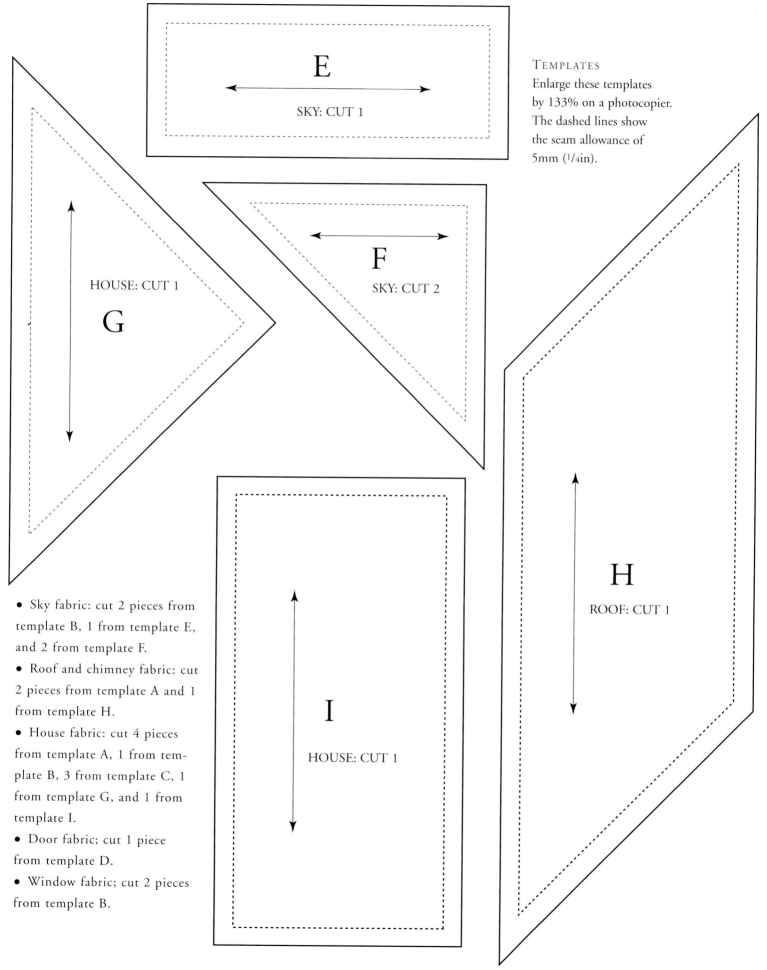

E
SKY: CUT 1

TEMPLATES
Enlarge these templates
by 133% on a photocopier.
The dashed lines show
the seam allowance of
5mm (1/4in).

HOUSE: CUT 1
G

F
SKY: CUT 2

H
ROOF: CUT 1

I
HOUSE: CUT 1

• Sky fabric: cut 2 pieces from
template B, 1 from template E,
and 2 from template F.
• Roof and chimney fabric: cut
2 pieces from template A and 1
from template H.
• House fabric: cut 4 pieces
from template A, 1 from template B, 3 from template C, 1
from template G, and 1 from
template I.
• Door fabric; cut 1 piece
from template D.
• Window fabric; cut 2 pieces
from template B.

Retirement Card

*I*F SOMEONE YOU KNOW is moving on to pastures new – retiring, changing jobs, or leaving to have a baby – this oriental sashiko design will wish them well. Chrysanthemums and water are often combined in Chinese imagery, because anyone drinking water into which chrysanthemum petals have fallen is supposed to live for a thousand years. So, whatever new life your colleague is going on to, this card will wish him or her a long and happy one! Silk seems just the right kind of fabric to use as the background of the design; choose the colour of your silk first, then find thin card in a colour that complements it for mounting the final piece. The card can then be framed as an everlasting memento.

Materials

- *28 x 18cm (11 x 7in) piece of pale aquamarine silk dupion*
- *28 x 18cm (11 x 7in) piece of curtain interlining*
- *Coton à broder in dark turquoise and two shades of copper*
- *54 x 28cm (21 x 11in) mid-turquoise card*
- *Fading pen*
- *Stick glue*
- *Pencil*
- *Craft knife*

TIP

Use a fading pen rather than a water-soluble pen for tracing this design, so that you don't have to wet the silk to remove the marks – silk isn't always colourfast.

OPPOSITE: *Chinese imagery and Japanese sashiko stitching combine to give this card an Oriental feel. Sashiko stitching is just a variation of ordinary quilting; it consists of large running stitches worked in a contrasting colour to the background fabric.*

Making the Retirement Card

1 Enlarge the design on page 125 by 110%. Lay the design down on a flat surface and position the rectangle of silk over it so that there is an even border at each side of the design. Trace all the lines of the design onto the silk with a fading pen.

2 Position the silk on top of the rectangle of interlining and baste the two layers together around the design.

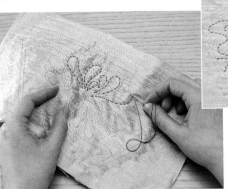

3 Using the darker copper coton à broder, begin stitching the main petals of the design in sashiko stitch – a long, even running stitch in which the stitches are roughly twice as long as the gaps between them. Use a random mixture of dark and light copper thread to stitch the different petals of the chrysanthemum. INSET: Now thread your needle with the turquoise coton à broder and stitch the lines of the water, keeping the curves smooth and even.

4 Stitch the inner border line in light copper, and the outer line in dark copper; keep the corners crisp. When all the stitching is complete, remove the basting. Leave the stitched design for a day or so until the traced lines have disappeared completely (this will happen faster if you put the stitched design in a sunny place such as a window-ledge).

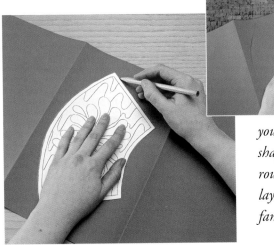

5 Fold the piece of card into three to create a long card that opens at the bottom. Score the creases lightly to make folding easier. Cut around the shape of the design on your original tracing or photocopy, and position this fan shape on the centre front of the middle panel; trace lightly round the shape in pencil. INSET: Unfold the card and lay it on a cutting surface; use a craft knife to cut a fan-shaped aperture 5mm (1/4in) outside the drawn line.

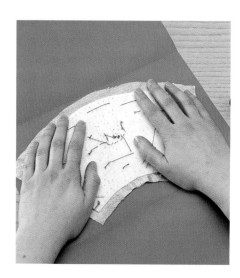

6 Trim the fabric to within 2cm (3/4in) of the stitched border all around. Trim the interlining back to just outside the stitching line.

7 Spread a little stick glue round the edges of the aperture on the wrong side of the card. Position the shape, right side out, in the aperture so that there is an even border of fabric all around the stitching. Spread glue around the edges of the bottom flap and fold it over to conceal the back of the embroidery. Your card is now complete.

TEMPLATE
Enlarge this template by
110% on a photocopier.

Index

AUTHOR'S ACKNOWLEDGEMENTS
Many thanks to Jenny Coleman, as she will be by the time this book is published, whose excellent stitching can be seen in the patchwork ball, the celtic knotwork picture and the pram quilt.

PUBLISHER'S ACKNOWLEDGEMENTS
With grateful thanks to Maggie Aldred, Loryn Birkholtz, Dawn Butcher, Anthony Duke, Claire Graham, Jon and Barbara Stewart and Janet Swarbrick for all their help.